God Didn't
Make Us
to Hate Us

God Didn't Make Us to Hate Us

40 Devotions to Liberate Your Faith from Fear and Reconnect with Joy

REV. LIZZIE McMANUS-DAIL

A TARCHERPERIGEE BOOK

tarcherperigee

an imprint of Penguin Random House LLC
1745 Broadway, New York, NY 10019
penguinrandomhouse.com

Most TarcherPerigee books are available at special quantity discounts for bulk purchase for sales
promotions, premiums, fundraising, and educational needs. Special books or book excerpts also
can be created to fit specific needs. For details, write SpecialMarkets@penguinrandomhouse.com.

Interior art: Flowers © Koliadzynka Iryna / Shutterstock

BOOK DESIGN BY KRISTIN DEL ROSARIO

Library of Congress Cataloging-in-Publication Data has been applied for.

ISBN 9780593850879 (hardcover)
ISBN 9780593850886 (ebook)

Printed in the United States of America
1   3   5   7   9   10   8   6   4   2

The authorized representative in the EU for product safety and compliance is
Penguin Random House Ireland, Morrison Chambers, 32 Nassau Street,
Dublin D02 YH68, Ireland, https://eu-contact.penguin.ie.

For Jonathan,
who introduced himself to me,
standing by the baptismal font,
with only an inkling of what this might foreshadow,

and for the beloved babes of God
who trusted me enough to ask the unspeakable questions,

and for everyone brave enough to believe
that God can be bigger than the boxes we were sold.

This is my love letter to you.

Thank you for persisting.

Gloria in excelsis Deo.

CONTENTS

INTRODUCTION   ix

PART I
Reimagining God 1

1. A Chaotic God   3
2. We Were Born Homesick   7
3. Fool's Gold   11
4. God Is More Like Music   16
5. God Gave You That Beautiful Body on Purpose   20
6. Eve's Question   25
7. Who Told You That You Are Naked?   31

PART II
Redeeming the Bible 37

8. Sarah Laughed at God, and God Liked It   39
9. Hagar, the Enslaved Woman Who Named God   44
10. Joseph's Fabulous Couture Coat   50
11. The Brutality of Mercy   56
12. Is It Exodus? Or Is It Texas?   61
13. Jubilee: God's Justice Is God's Joy   66
14. The Spiritual Discipline of Joy   70
15. Hannah Wanted a Baby but Found Her Voice   74
16. Born in Dazzling Darkness   80

PART III

Liberating Jesus 87

17. Mother of God, Dethroner of Dragons 89
18. Joseph and the Courage to Not Be the Main Character 95
19. Backwoods Empire 100
20. Jesus Loves a Sloppy Disco 104
21. Being Born Again Is About Being a Baby 109
22. The Tenacity of a Bleeding Woman 114
23. God Loves Us Bigger 119
24. Baptizing the Gender-Fringe 122
25. A God You Can Kick in the Shins 128
26. A Drag Queen Messiah 132
27. Judas Got His Feet Washed, Too 137
28. Breastfeeding the Body of Christ 142
29. God's Own Body 147
30. The Cross Was a Weapon 152
31. You Will Know Him by Broken Bread 157
32. Doubting, Faithful Thomas 162
33. Things We Cannot Heal 167

PART IV

The Great Hereafter 171

34. Hell on Earth 175
35. Bundled, Burned, Delivered 180
36. The Kin-dom of Heaven 185
37. God Is Offensively Generous 191
38. God Is a Bonkers Gardener 196
39. Sent Forth from Revelation to Revolution 201
40. The Great Vigil of Easter 205

ACKNOWLEDGMENTS 211
NOTES 214

The air was thick with that airplane hum: a sound that muffles and feels over-bright all at once. My mother had given me the window seat. I pressed my nose against the glass, the butter-yellow clouds outside stretching to the horizon.

I was in heaven; I wanted to see the angels.

I think I was maybe five years old. It wasn't my first time on a plane, but it is the time I remember as my first, likely in one of the many cross-country moves that creased my early childhood. The priest had told us heaven was full of fluffy white clouds and angels singing and playing harps. Or maybe it was my Sunday school teacher who said that. Or a television program. Somewhere in my Catholic upbringing—the only consistent thread in my early days—*someone* had told me there were angels way up here, in the sky, and I was determined to see them.

But all I saw, for miles and miles, was nothing but butter-yellow clouds. It felt like I waited for hours. Now that I'm a mother to a toddler, I suspect it lasted five minutes. But it ended the same way it always seems to end with toddlers: with a question.

"Mommy, why can't I see the angels?"

I remember my mom chuckled, exhaustion and amusement

bubbling up as she explained we weren't in heaven, exactly. Heaven was not a place we could fly to. "But isn't it beautiful all the same?" she asked.

I mean, it was beautiful. But it was not heaven.

This was my first deconstruction, I suppose. My first disillusionment. It was the first time something I had been told was true of God turned out to be . . . not necessarily false, but more complex than what I thought or had been taught. It was a little soul-crushing, if I'm honest, to discover that something I had imagined to be so simple and pure was actually made up of atoms and hydrogen rather than perfect pearly gates.

Deconstruction is a word that is increasingly being used by a movement of people questioning the rigid religious beliefs that were handed to them, unraveling what is useful and true from what is deceptive and exploitative. I want to be careful to lay no claim to defining the term for all people. But for me, this moment was the first of many in which what I thought was the right and faithful way to look for God was turned on its head. It was a moment wherein I felt lied to, and while I doubt the priests and teachers who told me angels lived in the clouds were consciously trying to deceive a little girl, that didn't stop this little girl from grieving her ticket to heaven. Many of the deconstruction moments that have come after that have been hard, and with *much* higher stakes than heaven's location—but none have been as crushing to my innocent hope as when I was five and learned I could not spend a journey between Raleigh and Los Angeles listening to the heavenly hosts on their cloudy thrones.

Since then, I have grown, left, and re-found the church, been ordained an Episcopal priest, and become a mother. I have tasted the bitter and beautiful waters of a baptism that keeps me yoked to a God and an institution that has broken my heart a million times. I have heard the church tell me I was not good enough, I was not wanted, I was crazy, I was fundamentally corrupt. And I have watched the church stand by in the face of horrific abuse.

And yet, to quote Martin Luther, one of the most famous (and famously problematic) people ever to deconstruct his faith: *Here I stand. I can do no other.*

Because faith *is* still beautiful, all the same.

And I know this because somehow, in those early days of hearing stories about angels and looking for them in the clouds and meeting them in forever the most unexpected places, I came to know something fundamental about God and God's character that no disillusioning of the church could thieve from me:

God did not make us to hate us.

God did not dream up the color yellow and craft the scientific art of making butter from milk and whimsically birth cumulus clouds just to . . . disdain a little girl who misunderstood the cosmic structure.

God did not count the hairs on our heads or the stars that would hang in the sky over billions of years just to resentfully accept desperate people begging to be spared from brutal torment.

I know this because maybe heaven isn't a pit stop between Raleigh and LA, but heaven *is* all around us. Breaking in and barreling down walls and peeping up like dandelions in the asphalt. God would not be so creative and wily and beautiful all at the same time if God's desire was punishment.

Maybe this belief is ego, maybe it is a gift from the Spirit, maybe it is both. But this abiding sense of God's desire for all of us has been a shield for me that I now want to extend to you. I want to lay it out as an invitation and an answer to the thousands of questions I get online as a priest that ask: Why does God hate me so much?

I also really believe that there is great potential in being disillusioned, painful as it may be to suddenly and irrevocably see the world so differently. To paraphrase my friend Erin Lane, is not being disillusioned, being set free from our illusions, the point of faith? Isn't there actually a super famous story in the Bible about scales falling from a faithful, God-fearing, earnest man's eyes as the God he had always worshipped stepped in with a real flourish and said, *You are looking for me in all the wrong places and in so doing, you are hurting me and my people?* (Spoiler alert: there is—Acts 9, the calling of Saint Paul, author of about half the New Testament.)

Over and over throughout Christian history, scales have fallen from our collective eyes, and we, the faithful and the skeptical, have deconstructed. Sometimes this was called reformation, sometimes this was called schism, sometimes this was called sin. It's a mixed bag, this millennia-long endeavor of the great Group Project that is Christianity. But I remain convinced of the power inlaid in the falling of the scales from our eyes as we behold a brutal new truth, hard fought for. We might be uncertain what can be won, worried it won't be worth it. But what might happen if we were all willing to let this truth set us free?

Because all bad theology, in my humble opinion, keeps us chained in systems of oppression. All bad theology has its root in thinking God hates us: homophobia and transphobia, racism and misogyny, ableism and classism all stem from an anxiety created by the idea that God *hates* us and that we must repair this breach by receiving the forgiveness He offers, begrudgingly.

This theology fundamentally communicates: *You are not safe. You are never safe.* So when you get a modicum of safety by following all the rules and living the "right" kind of life, you must hoard this safety, arm yourself, and prepare to confront anyone who threatens this battleship you have secured yourself within. Because this safety is tenuous, and the way you keep yourself safe in your right life is ensuring other people know *their* lives are wrong. Everyone wants to be safe, and everyone wants to know how to *stay* safe, and the result is this: so many people feel fundamentally unsafe because they have been told, by the same people who make them casseroles when Grandma dies and who are there when they are brave enough to say they need to get sober, that the creator of the universe doesn't like them.

You learn that God is merciful, but you don't deserve that mercy. You are not fundamentally wanted for who you are. Your body is a problem you must conquer. You can only find safety by following a version of God that looks an awful lot like whichever bully has a grasp on power in your particular church or community.

So how do we melt away the fear?

I believe it begins here: by looking at the heavens, and looking at the dandelion in the cracks, and looking at scripture, and looking at God, and trying an older and wilder way of trust. It begins by saying: *God did not make me to hate me; God made me to love me. God made me out of desire. God made me out of joy.*

God is not so small-minded or vindictive as to make people in order to just . . . hate them. I mean, look at the sheer multitude of galaxies in the universe. The membranes of butterfly wings. The way a toddler's teeth make the most crooked and sublime smile when they laugh. The dreamer-upper of these things isn't an asshole. I just don't buy it. The Bible doesn't sell it, either; while full of challenging and complex stories that do dip into the lament and wrath of God, scripture on the whole has an undercurrent *and* over-arc of God's delight in God's people.

Becoming a mom solidified this conviction for me. I love my daughter more than my hands and hopes can hold—and God loves us infinitely more. There's just no logic, then, even considering the higher and more mysterious ways of God, in the idea that God hates us.

And yet so much of modern theology from the last few centuries is built on this idea that God will eternally punish or harm or torment people. For not being Christian nationalists. For being queer. For having consensual, beautiful sex. For caring about the environment. (And that's a non-exhaustive list.)

As a priest, this troubles me greatly. I have had the immense, intimate privilege of walking alongside people of every theological background—people of many different races, people from thriving families and families rife with trauma and pain, people of many nationalities and sexualities and gender identities, people who have grown up in liberal northeastern cities and rural Texan towns—and so, so many of us are so, so afraid. I have witnessed firsthand over and over how long-lasting and damaging this embedded fear is—in the way we relate to our bodies, our partners, our children, our communities, and our God.

I've seen people afraid to love and be loved because they think they're not worthy of such care. I've seen caregivers terrified of raising their children in a loving church community because they don't want to re-create the traumatic experiences they had as children in church. I've seen queer people in flourishing relationships who still wrestle with wondering if they deserve to be loved. I've seen women (including myself) who wondered what they "did" to "deserve" violence they thought was handed down from God through people. And I have seen, over and over, a resignation to suffering formed as a reaction to a vengeful deity out to punish us.

Whether we grew up in churches that proclaimed divine retribution from the pulpit regularly or whether we "only" encountered this theology splashed on what feels like every other billboard in America, this bad theology that proclaims God hates us is in the water we all drink from in American Christianity.

But this idea that God *hates* us is not the root of Christianity or the heart of Christ.

So . . . what is?

I am deeply convicted that God's heart for us is and always has been to *live with* us. God made us for and out of joy. As my best friend Nora said the day my daughter was baptized: *being naked in the Garden was the original plan.* This is a key that unlocks so much bad theology, but even more important, knowing that God made us for joy unclenches the chokehold that cynicism and despair have on us.

If God made us—all of us, with tummies and wrinkles and libido and hearts that break and burst with life—for joy, then imagine how joyful life with God could be. If we fully accept this godly delight, who might we become? Who are we already if we let ourselves meet ourselves without malice or intent to harm? What freedom is already here? And what might be even more beautiful than it already is?

With this book, I humbly offer a small place we might begin. A place where we can deconstruct the myths that have been spun out of our faith and return to life with God. A place where we can prune branches back to give the vineyard fresh air, to let the good fruit grow without being throttled by weeds that whisper, *Don't taste too sweet.* I'm not here to promise certainty or answers, but I hope to invite us into the plot of the best mystery novel ever composed: the mystery of living life with the source of life.

To that end, this book is divided into four sections, each of which aims to debunk a common myth about Christianity and replace it with a true mystery we can explore and learn from. These forty reflections come from a blend of ancient theology, modern mom life, and a long love affair with the Bible as a priest and Christian. They come from my own disillusionment and enchantment with God, through conversations with theologians, scholars, friends, and parishioners—all of whom have taught me so much.

I've written forty devotions because forty is a biblical number. The Israelites spent forty years wandering the desert, and Jesus spent forty days in the wilderness after his baptism, which is why the season of Lent lasts forty days (excluding Sundays). These devotions can be used during Lent, but they can also be used at any time. You can read the whole book in forty days, or four days, or forty weeks. How you use it is totally up to you. My goal is simply to break down big theological ideas into more digestible pieces to help you heal your church hurt and reconnect with a God worth worshipping.

I'll also conclude each chapter with a prayer. These prayers are in the first person plural—they say "we pray" rather than "I pray." (In my tradition, the Episcopal Church, we call this kind of prayer a *collect*, pronounced CALL-ekt. Yes, it's spelled just like the word *collect*, but Episcopalians like a fancy pronunciation, bless our hearts.) I've chosen this format for two main reasons.

First, I want to move away from an overemphasis on individualism in Christianity. *We* acknowledge *we* are part of a body of people. Our belief is *ours*, as a collective. We will not always agree.

We definitely have not always gotten along. But we are knitted together, all the same, and I believe what we pray in common helps remind us that our God holds us in common and communion and community, too. And: God did make *you* and *me* but ultimately made *us* to delight in *us* together, as a body of people and as people *with* God.

Second, I know it can be terribly lonely to deconstruct—to walk away from a faith community you have always known or to stay in a community but feel like you're swimming upstream. But you are not alone. God is and always has been and always will be with you. And as you say the same prayers as all the other readers of this book, albeit at different places and different times, you are threaded together with people whom you may never meet (and some, perhaps, you will meet or already know!). They, too, are on a parallel journey. I want that to be clear in the very grammar of these prayers. We are not alone. We get free together.

In the spirit of the late, great Audre Lorde, I hope the tools in these prayers and devotions will help us not just dismantle the master's house but also find an older and wiser and wilder way of living with God. A way to dive into what the mystic Carmelite nun Saint Teresa of Avila called an "interior castle" that can pour out into a kinder, gentler, and more loving world.

A Garden way, you might say. Harkening back to that original plan. Eating fruit and being together without shame. Staring at sunsets and sunrises and everything in between and saying, as God says in Genesis 1: *That's good.*

PART I

Reimagining God

MYTH: God is our Father, therefore male power is God.

MYSTERY: God is a Holy Trinity—three distinct persons not in competition with each other and uniquely one God, whose very essence is community.

We often pray to God our Father. This is a good thing, as it is, you know, literally how Jesus taught us to pray in Matthew 6 and Luke 11. "Our Father" remains a sacred and important prayer. But when we uncritically apply this one description of God across the whole of scripture, and our entire prayer lives, and use it as a metaphor for what godliness looks like in the world, we end up boxing our Triune God into human, masculine fatherhood. God is our Father, but God is not your dad. Nor is God a system that only benefits masculine-looking and feminine-demoralizing power.

Feminist theologian Mary Daly wrote in 1973, "If God is male, then the male is God." We have seen this come to bear in our own day. As Kristin Kobes Du Mez outlines in her book *Jesus and John Wayne*, many forms of evangelical Christianity have made following Christ synonymous with a violent, white, America-first-and-only idolatry of masculinity. This is not who Our Father is. Jesus isn't asking us to pray to Rambo, or John Wayne, or any emperor who sits in the government, or even our dads, as problematic or tender as they may be. By calling God "Father," Jesus is naming a *relationship* that he shares within Godself as part of the Holy Trinity. I don't think you or I need to drop "Father" from our language for God, but I do think we are, at best, missing out on the rest of God when we only look for God in fatherly imagery. God is also not just our Father; God is Father, Son, *and* Holy Spirit. Three persons, one God—our Trinity, whose art is heaven.

And also? In the Bible itself *God* does not exclusively refer to Godself in masculine imagery or pronouns. Sometimes God refers to Himself as "She," and sometimes She refers to Herself as "They," and sometimes They do not use any kind of gendered, human-bound imagery at all to describe Themself. This is not some newfangled idea, either. Our spiritual ancestors—from Clement of Alexandria, to Augustine of Hippo, to John Chrysostom, to Anselm of Canterbury, and *many* others—have often articulated an understanding of God as containing many gendered aspects. It is actually quite an old-fashioned thing to think that God is bigger than gender.

We cut our own imagination and relationship with God off at the knees when we see the image of divine authority as merely a projection of human power. To fall in love with God over and over is not to mythologize our own earthly kingdoms, but to behold the mystery that the creator of the universe disrupts in those kingdoms by walking through the back gate, by hanging out in the side alley, by creating something wild and unpredictable and gentle out of chaotic nothing. So let's move from the myths about God into the mystery of faith.

A Chaotic God

. . . .

When God began to create the heavens and the
earth, the earth was complete chaos, and darkness covered the face of the deep, while a wind
from God swept over the face of the waters.

GENESIS 1:1–2

Our story begins in chaos. In the fathomless, dark deep. But God
brings order and life to this chaos in the evenings and mornings
that follow, separating light from darkness and sea from land, and
putting creatures upon the earth in what feels like neat array.

God disciplines chaos into creation as a wind.

And, as you know if you live anywhere near enormous tur-
bines like the ones I have come to know on the plains of Texas,
wind isn't exactly . . . orderly. Wind is chaotic. It rips tablecloths
off of pristine backyard party tables. It ruins a good hair day. It can
knock down houses and communities. When harnessed, it can
power cities—but the wind is never, ever tamed. Only funneled,
for a time.

And it is as this chaotic wind that God first moves over that
fathomless deep.

In the thousands of years since this story was first told by firelight under a bottomless black sky, we have often imagined God created the world this way because God loves order. Because God is the great discipliner of disarray.

I think the notion of God knowing and creating the order of things is sensible, calming even. Surely *someone* knows the exact dimensions of the ocean and why the platypus exists and where all my misplaced socks have gone—why not God? But it also feels awfully unimaginative and limiting to want to order chaos. It feels like when my toddler takes a crayon and colors all outside the lines. Because I know the purpose of lines on a page, I want her to color *in* the lines. As a grumbly grown-up, I want to show her that a crayon is made for coloring on paper and paper is made for us to draw on. But she is unashamedly and beautifully discovering the feel of colored wax in her hands, experiencing the divine moment of seeing something made by her motion, and discovering what paper is—for the first time.

And of course there is an order to this. She learned first that her hands were her own to move. Then she learned to grasp a crayon. And someday (God willing) she will learn that we *hang* art on the walls, we don't *draw* art on the walls (without permission).

Order is good. It is not that I think God lacks order. I just think God's ordering is in the form of wind. And we neglect the wildness of wind at our own peril.

God is the wind over the deep. God is the mom who knows a toddler does not yet comprehend crayon and paper as separate substances, so She will lovingly guide the way, but not without some truly spectacular splatter art first. And so to encounter God, untamed and true and old and holy, is to lay down our need for control, our need for God to fit within the lines on our coloring pages. We have to let God wield the paintbrushes that have always been in Her hand.

And the thing about the divine wind in Genesis 1 is that it could also be translated as the "Spirit" or the "breath" of God. The Hebrew word here is *ruach*, a grammatically feminine noun. Some translations of Genesis 1 preserve that femininity, like womanist theologian Wilda C. Gafney's: "When beginning he, God, created the heavens and the earth, the earth was shapeless and formless and bleakness covered the face of the deep, while the Spirit of God, she, fluttered over the face of the waters." *Ruach* is used many, many times in the Bible—including the part of the Creation story where God breathes the breath of life into the earth-creatures He makes—the people we call Adam and Eve. You were created out of the wildness that is the She-Spirit. You were made out of the dust that gathered in the wake of all this chaos and all this creating, all this land emerging and ocean tide flowing out.

You were made wild.

The wildness in us—the desire to know God, to be free, to seek love and do the unbelievably risky thing of sharing love—is as foundational as breathing, because it is the very breath of God in us that has oxygenated us from the beginning.

Of course there must be order to our lives, and order to the world! But this order does not need to be so bound by fear-fueled lines that we do not make room for the toddlers in our lives—or the toddlers that are still within all of us—to play and learn. The challenge and gift of leaning into a liberated life with God is learning to trust that even in the chaos, God is creating something new.

. . . .

Wind over the deep,
You breathed us into being
and still,
You are always closer than our next breath.

Nurture the holy wildness in us,
so that when we meet You,
in the setting of the sun, or in the coming tide,
we are not afraid
but ready to welcome You,
untamed, unbridled,
holy and wild.

Small but unconfined,
we cry to You:
Spirit over the deep,
Author of the deep,
with us in the deep.
Amen.

We Were Born Homesick

. . . .

Dear friends, let us love one another, for love comes
from God. Everyone who loves has been born of
God and knows God. . . . No one has ever seen
God; but if we love one another, God lives in us and
his love is made complete in us.

1 JOHN 4:7, 12 (NIV)

"If all goes well, she should be screaming."

I can't remember if it was a midwife or a birthing book or a
friend who said that, but I knew: when my daughter was born, if
all was well, she would be screaming. Throat-raw howling.

When the doctors lowered the surgical drape for me to see
them extract her from my exhausted womb via Caesarean section,
I felt cleaved in two. Love split me open as they took my heart
from my gut. But then I was in and out of focus, and the nurse was
stroking my hair, and my husband was over by the doctors—all
because my baby was quiet.

Too quiet. And purple.

And then, mercifully, she began to scream. I have never been
so grateful for the sounds of agony in my life.

When we are born, if all goes well, we should be screaming.
The only thing a baby has ever known is the dark safety of a

womb, and now they are catapulted into the brutal light of the world. Maybe this is why so many people have said we are born in sin. Birth is terrifying, and we tend to label scary things or things we don't understand as "sin."

Or maybe it's because birth is so connected with women and sexuality. Despite the fact that birthing people's bodies are life-cradling wonders, our society is so uncomfortable with the realities of the reproductive process that we've created a variety of awful names to call women who engage in it in ways we don't approve of. We associate birth with sinful femininity so strongly that we laud birthing pains as part of Eve's punishment.

This is such a wayward definition of sin. Sin is not, as my colleague Rev. Kelli Joyce puts it, "fun stuff you're not allowed to do, and especially with your body, *especially* if your body is not the kind of body that the church wants it to be." This is what I think most people mean when they say *sin*, but over and over, the Bible shows us that sin is more fundamental than "fun stuff you're not allowed to do." Sin is anything that separates us from God and from one another. Sin is the *nothing* in the face of God's abundance. And I certainly felt the encroaching nothing, the bottomless fear of *what if* . . . on that operating table.

But sometimes, I think we use the word *sin* when what we really mean is *death*, and by death, we mean the inescapable reality of our humanity. Of our limits. We are merely human, and only God is God. And sin and death are connected in the Christian tradition, but they are not the same. In that moment when my baby was too quiet, I knew death was threatening all that was good and right and holy in that space. But was my baby being born *in* sin? Or was I reckoning with my humanity now that she was not a part of my body?

My friend Sus Long offers this alternative: "We were not born in sin—we were born homesick." It's the opening line of the song "Born Homesick" from her band Hardworker's EP *The Awful Rowing*.

My baby was not born in sin. She was born homesick. When I finally got to hold her, hours later, and put her to my breast, where she knew how to eat despite never having used her mouth to eat before, we were not quite one flesh again, but we were not lonely for each other. Strangers, but blood. Kin-bound. Soul-tied. And I will never feed her to eternal fullness like God will, but in some ways her homesickness was sated.

My love for her is from God, but only God loves perfectly. My job is to receive that perfect love and do my best to live in that love, extend that love, give that love, knowing I never will love as God does. This is what I hear in this phrase "We were born homesick." We are born, and remain, hungry. Consumed with a desire to be where we knew we were safe and fed, where it was dark and warm, and where we were not overwhelmed with being alive in an enormous and often heartless world.

We are born wanting. And the wanting lingers. The wanting haunts.

And the only antidote, really, to this wanting—to this deep fear of not being enough, of not being worthy, of not being in control or able to shield your children or yourself from harm, this fear of *incompleteness*, this homesickness we cannot name—is God. It is to realize that God loves us in our limits, and that God is with us, always. For when we love, we are born of God, and everyone born is born in God's unlimited love.

We love and worship a wild God whose ways are not our ways, whose presence with us is ultimately a mystery. But even as the reasons why we're left screaming or sad or lonely are not always discernible or even divine, we *can* trust that our wild God is where we came from and to whom we will return.

My baby, thanks be to God, did begin to scream, and I was rolled out of that hospital with her in my arms. I know not everyone is so lucky. And my task is to love her as fully as I can, for as long as I can, fervently praying and pleading and trusting that someday—God willing, long from now—all of us will be home together, where the wanting does not haunt but is sated.

. . . .

O God,
  our hearts are restless until they rest in You.
  Open forth our longing for You,
  give us courage to see the truth of who we are,
  and where we are sick from want for things that
          are not You,
  and when we are afraid because we think You
          are not there,
  remind us that Your love is perfect and Your
          love is sufficient
  and Your love is for all of us, always.
  For You are our homemaker,
  our home,
  and our homing.
  Amen.

Fool's Gold

. . . .

Jesus answered, "The first is, 'Hear, O Israel: the
Lord our God, the Lord is one; you shall love the
Lord your God with all your heart and with all
your soul and with all your mind and with all your
strength.' The second is this, 'You shall love your
neighbor as yourself.' There is no other commandment greater than these."

MARK 12:29–31

I have often heard it said that you don't know true love until you
become a parent. I have also heard my fellow Christians say you
need to love God more than anyone else—more than your friends,
your spouse, even your child.

So which is it: I didn't know love until I became a mom? Or my
love for my child—my earth-shattering, wall-climbing, lion's-
teeth-facing love for my child—is too much?

In some ways, it is true that becoming a parent taught me about
love. Giving birth cleaved me in two and doubled my love for my
baby, for my husband, and for this weary world. But to say I didn't
really know love until then feels . . . shallow? Dismissive? For it
was a great love between me and my husband that brought her

into the world, and that love was born of companionship and solidarity and deep mutual care. It seems to me that there are all kinds
of love that, like parenthood, we don't know until we know them.
There's the love of true, deep friendship. The love of a vocation
that fills you with purpose. The love of a place that becomes home,
perhaps unexpectedly. The love of a community that is a family.

I think the *actual* problem is that bargain-bin theology loves to
reduce holy mystery to a sound bite. Categorize and reduce the
mess into a clean hierarchy: love God, then love others, and be a
good person by checking these boxes. Sometimes I think the "love
God first" talk wants us to love our family and friends (and maybe
enemies?) with 49 percent of our love, but love God with 51 percent of our love, to make sure God gets the biggest slice of pie. This
is a ridiculous way to think about love, and a ridiculous way to
think about God. It turns the golden rule into fool's gold, something shiny but fleeting, unable to last because it isn't of a substance made to endure wear and tear. True love that comes from
God cannot be reduced to percentages. As novelist Lisa Kleypas
says, "A heart [can] make as much room as love needed."

Because the absolutely wild thing about God is that God knows
all of this love already. God is *in* all of this love already. Because
God *is* all of this love already!

My love for others—the ferocious willingness I have to go anywhere and do anything for my child, for my husband, for my
friends—this is love that is never, ever outside of God, because
there is nowhere my love or being can go that is outside of God.
True love that comes from God is abundant, not subtractive. It
makes room for more and more love. God is expansive, and so
love, which is of and from God, is also expansive.

Loving my baby, and my husband, and my dad, and my best

friends—none of these loves negate or compete with my love for God. In fact, God's greatest commandment—to love God and love our neighbor as ourselves—forms a kind of trinity of love: love of God, love of neighbor, love of self. You cannot have one of these without having the other two.

Self-love without neighbor-love is selfish, and can quickly boil into greed, abuse, entitlement, and violence.

Neighbor-love without self-love—showing kindness to others without letting them show kindness back to us—is paradoxically egotistical, because if we think we can love our neighbors without also receiving love or care, we're saying we're like God. God does not need us, but we need love, from God and our neighbors. We also need to be willing to receive that love—for our own benefit, but also to let our neighbors benefit from following the golden commandment. If we don't ever let other people love us, we're depriving them of a chance to fully live into their Christian call to love *their* neighbors.

God-love without neighbor-love idolatrously reduces God to an absentee landlord, not the Creator and Redeemer of all people—*all* people. Inconvenient, needy, frustrating, cruel, hapless, gorgeous, caring, golden people: all made in God's image.

We need all three—love of God, love of neighbor, and love of self—to fulfill the greatest commandment. Loving God *requires* us to love people. As 1 John 4:7, 12 says, "Let's love each other, because love is from God. . . . If we love each other, God remains in us and his love is made perfect in us" (CEB).

Sometimes God feels like a blanket that envelops me, and the world, and everyone I encounter. Like the exposure settings are both over-bright and perfectly warm, like I can see everyone and everything and our threads of connection.

At other times, the despair is enormous. God can feel far away, or impossible to grasp. And when we cannot feel that love, when the despair is too much, when we are full of rage that God could *let this happen* . . . our task is maybe not to love God in some big, holy, sky-reaching praise but to love the people God gave us right here. Love them imperfectly, inevitably. But love them. Love ourselves. And let this love ground us.

Because that love is God saying: *I am with you, always. Even here. Even now.*

For God's love for us is greater than the love parents have for their children, and greater than the love friends have for each other, and greater than the love we share even here—because God *is* that love, and so much more.

. . . .

Lover of souls,
    You have wrapped us in Your infinite affection.
    From our unremembered infancy to the
        moments that weigh us down now,
    You have always loved us,
    completely.

When we feel like love is a scarcity to be measured,
    doled out in small sums, to keep the lock on our
        hearts securely fastened,
    unfurl our fingers in the way only You can
    and remind us that Your love is not counted in
        cups or days,
    but in the infinite, borderless expanse

of all the rooms, in all the universe,
and more.

And when we feel like we have no love left to
        spare,
    draw us to collapse in Your arms,
    kiss our foreheads,
    and remind us:
    Your love can bear all things, even when we
        cannot.

Author of Love, who believes and hopes and
        endures,
    Hold us now, and evermore.

Amen.

· 4 ·

God Is More Like Music

....

> Likewise the Spirit helps us in our weakness, for
> we do not know how to pray as we ought, but that
> very Spirit intercedes with groanings too deep for
> words. And God, who searches hearts, knows
> what is the mind of the Spirit, because the Spirit
> intercedes for the saints according to the will
> of God.
>
> ROMANS 8:26–27

One of the wildest things about the end of life is what we remember. When I spent a year as a chaplain in a continuous-care retirement community, I walked alongside sweet old ladies (and a few mean old ladies), veterans, grieving widows and widowers, and women who were finally free. I knew ninety-year-olds who could run literal circles around me. But I spent the most time in the memory and skilled-care units, where the only things running were the seemingly hundreds of TVs in every room. A lot of things go at the end; many of us become like small children again, crying for our mothers, mistaking children for long-dead parents, becoming irascible about change and dependent on routine. But some things seem to carve themselves into the stonework of our souls—things like music.

I love to sing, despite having more passion than talent for the enterprise, and once it got out that I could carry a tune, I was often asked by nurses to sing some of the gold-standard hymns as part of my pastoral visits in these units. Usually, I went for "Amazing Grace." And the wild part was that many people who could no longer speak, no longer say their own name, possibly not even recognize a single member of their family, *could still sing along to this song.* And even if they couldn't sing, they would give some sign of knowing it—stirring from their deep-minded reverie to give me a pat on the hand or humming tunelessly along.

Saint Augustine is credited with saying, "Singing is praying twice." And while often we think of prayer as a specific act in a specific time and place, maybe where we get down on our knees or hold hands, when we bow our heads, close our eyes, and talk to God—I think that, ultimately, no matter where or when or how it happens, prayer is the deepest ache of our heart being given voice. Sometimes that voice is only in our heads, but sometimes it is in *music*, in a language of sound and sense and lyrics. Trying to describe what music does to us is like trying to explain why we as a species need water: there are words, sure, but there is also a full-body hunger caked with memory of the refreshment it gives to our souls.

God is a lot like music.

We have so many metaphors and images in the Bible to describe God, but the language we use the most in Christianity is that of Holy Trinity: Father, Son, and Holy Spirit. Three persons, one God; three names, one name. It's a mind-scramble for sure. To describe the Holy Trinity is, necessarily, to employ an insufficient metaphor. Saint Patrick reportedly likened the Trinity to the shamrocks with their three leaves but one stem. Sunday school teachers everywhere talk about the way water can be liquid, vapor, or ice but is still always equally water. Sometimes the Trinity is likened to the way we as people contain multiple identities like mother, sister, and daughter.

These metaphors serve their use, sure. The problem is, though, that as a mother, sister, and daughter, I often feel at war with myself because of the competing needs among these identities. Outside of lab experiments, water cannot be liquid, vapor, and ice all at once, even if all three are present in a lovely steaming sauna in Iceland. Shamrocks are cute, but those three leaves are distinct from each other.

And God is not in competition within Godself, ever. God is everywhere as the whole of God all at once, not sending the Son to run errands while the Spirit cooks dinner. And God—Father, Son, and Holy Spirit—is not distinct from Godself. (Need an aspirin yet?)

So what metaphor *can* we use?

I return to my old patients and the way they knew God without being able to say a cognizant prayer or even the word God. We know God in the language God gives us that already surpasses metaphor and speech: music.

To get technical, as Dr. Jeremy Begbie taught me in divinity school, we know the Trinity like we know a *chord*. A chord is when multiple notes are played at the same time—in this case, three notes. Each note resonates with its own sound and tone, but the sounds of the individual notes are inextricable from the sound of the three notes together. The notes are a community, a nestled-in sound that is at once the sum of its parts, more than the sum of its parts, and its individual parts shining bright.

The Trinity is like this because the Trinity *is* community. God is inherently community. This is why we believe God does not create humans out of lack or need—because God does not have

need for companionship. God has God! And we, who are knitted
into the life and Body of God, are knitted into this community and
are challenged to sing our brightest and best notes such that they
make music with all of God's children in noncompetitive, glorify-
ing, and glorious harmony. Because true community in God feels
like really good music: it ebbs and flows, crescendos and decre-
scendos, and needs many different notes to be interesting.

And when we fail to make music, when our voices and bodies
fail us, when we choose to scream or be silent instead of sing?
God's music will find us. It will call us from the silence of lost
memory, ground us when we are lost, and beckon us home when
we are ready to sing with the heavenly chorus.

How sweet the sound.

. . . .

Amazing Grace,
 who taught our hearts to fear,
 and Grace who relieves our fears—
when we are lost,
 knit us back into Your fabric;
when we are in danger,
 remind us that we are never alone;
when we are tempted to think anyone is outside of
 Your creation,
 remind us we have no less days to sing Your praise
 in chorus, not as a solo;
for Your grace has brought us safe thus far,
 and Your grace will lead us home.
Amen.

· 5 ·

God Gave You That Beautiful Body on Purpose

....

God created humanity in God's own image,
in the divine image God created them.

GENESIS 1:27 (CEB)

"Can I talk to you for a second?" I asked, cupping my friend by the elbow.

She looked confused and nodded. A whole gaggle of us were visiting her mom's house for the night, taking an evening away from Mount Holyoke, our college. We were piling in the basement to watch a movie, dressed in our usual college comfies: leggings, slippers, and enormous "man sweaters" so thick they were like wearing a knitted blanket.

It was the leggings that had me worried. "Is it . . . is it okay that I'm wearing these around your mom?"

My friend blinked, bemused, before quickly nodding and smiling. "Yeah, of course!"

New England was a *revelation* to this Southern girl.

I don't often consider my Southern upbringing to be conservative; this is, perhaps, because the way the American South is portrayed by people not of the American South is rarely a full-color kind of picture. But the combination of growing up with a soft belly in the age of low-rise jeans and in a Christian culture that was a hair's breadth to the left of *I Kissed Dating Goodbye* meant I was equally panicked that my leggings were both unflattering *and* too sexy.

Purity culture told me I was so desirable I had to be contained. Beauty standards told me I was so undesirable I had to hate myself into thinness. Both engines of oppression wanted me smaller (and it was even worse for those who didn't have the same level of privilege I had as a cisgender, white teen).

The contradictions sliced two ways: by purity culture standards, any exposure of my body was an unacceptable and inevitable temptation for men to sin, and yet by the beauty standards of the early 2000s, my body was unacceptably unattractive and an inevitable disappointment to me no matter what I wore, ate, or did. Put these purity and beauty standards together, and you create an expectation of violence from men that women must both endure and somehow ignore.

Preying upon little girls' insecurities (and our mothers' fears) is a profitable enterprise. If the goalpost for beauty is ever moving, then the sales are ever growing.

Preying upon children's burgeoning curiosity and inevitable changes in their bodies establishes patterns of control and dominance early on in the minds of children. If we learn young to fear our own *body*—the one thing that is with us until we die—we will always be tempted to trust the voices of criticism outside of ourselves more than the voice of wisdom inside of ourselves.

Even with the unreconcilable dueling messages of *your body will never be attractive enough* and *your body will never be blameless enough*, somehow the message was clear: my body would never be *good* enough.

And that's how I felt—until I began to think about why I had a body to begin with.

God is wildly creative, after all. God made the giraffe and the solar eclipse. God did not *need* to make people, and God did not *need* to encase us in these bodies that are changing from the moment we first expand our lungs with breath. And yet our changeless God made us in such a way that we are, always, changing.

Interestingly enough, it is the very fact that we're always changing that forms the basis of the purity laws actually found in scripture. As my Old Testament professor Ellen Davis said when I was in divinity school, purity laws acknowledge that something in our bodies has changed. So when God commands a mikveh, or bath, after something like menstruation, it's not because the essential condition of a birthing body is a state of sinfulness. It is because something about that body has changed, and God cares about that change.

Having a period means my body has shed something that was designed for receiving life and now is to be returned to the earth. Sometimes, having a period has been a relief. Sometimes it has been a grief. Sometimes it has been a painful reminder of my vulnerability. Sometimes it just . . . is. But in all of these times, I have changed, in ways that could be small but that could also be enormous. And biblical purity laws reveal that God cares—*not* that God judges.

Bodies change all the time. And these changes are not the problem—they are, actually, as Rabbi Esther Hugenholtz notes, invitations to let transitions transform us, draw us deeper into our changeless God, and revel in our humanity.

God cares about the minutiae of my body. God sees the little things only I notice. God is not wrathful or condemning or even,

I think, concerned about these small and big changes, but God knows *transition needs care*. God knows when I need a moment to acknowledge my body, my only guaranteed lifelong companion, which God wove for me—for *me*! God knows when we need to pause and remember that even in this change, in this unfolding or expanding or loss, we are still made in God's own image.

But while the human body needs a divine tending-to, it is *not* a divine problem.

The human body unfolds the magic of a God who thinks ahead, a God who adorns our faces and sagging arms and hidden crevices with a map to mark all the belly laughs we've enjoyed and all the winters we have weathered. God expands us and shifts us and shrinks us and empties us and fills us. God made our bodies in all of their imperfections out of God's pleasure.

And, yes, bodies can change in ways that haunt us. We do not always trust or like our bodies. That's okay.

But having a body? Any kind of body? That is part of Christian life. We are not spiritual beings meant to rise above our mortal flesh. God made our bodies and said: *That is good*.

Our flesh was good enough for God to descend and dwell among us in a human body. The birthing body of a woman was good enough for God to descend down her birth canal, good enough to expel Christ himself in blood and water, in a place where animals ate. Out of Christ's own side on the cross both blood and water poured forth, just as happens in birth.

Those first earth-creatures, Eve and Adam, were naked in the Garden and unashamed. Nowhere in the text does it say that Eve was thin and lithe and blond or that Adam was acne-free and muscular. Rather, they spent all their time eating the plumpest fruits and naming animals, which means, to my imagining, that their bodies were shameless not because they were perfect but because they trusted God would not make something beautiful only for us to wish it took up less space.

·················

Let us pray to God to help us trust our oldest friends, our bodies:

> Womb of Life,*
>> You breathed life into us, knowing that our
>>> lungs would grow,
>> expanding over the years of deep breaths and
>>> gasping sighs—
>
> Help us breathe in: *My body is good enough*
>> and exhale: *Because You said so.*
>
> Help us breathe in: *My body is beautiful*
>> and exhale: *Because You made it.*
>
> Because You are the One who wove us, claimed us,
>> and birthed us.
>> Amen.

---

* I am indebted to the scholarship of Rev. Dr. Wilda C. Gafney for her interpretation of the tetragrammaton, the unpronounceable Most Holy Name of God, which is sometimes spelled out as YHWH. In her book *A Women's Lectionary for the Whole Church*, she "adopted the practice of choosing descriptive expressions for the name of God and other divine names and titles." She used over 120 such expressions, one of which I prayerfully use here: WOMB OF LIFE. (Wilda C. Gafney, "About the Translations," in *A Women's Lectionary for the Whole Church: Year W* [New York: Church Publishing, 2021], Kindle.)

· 6 ·

Eve's Question

· · · · · · · · · · · · · · · · ·

> So when the woman saw that the tree was good for
> food and that it was a delight to the eyes and that
> the tree was to be desired to make one wise, she
> took of its fruit and ate, and she also gave some to
> her husband, who was with her, and he ate. Then
> the eyes of both were opened, and they knew that
> they were naked, and they sewed fig leaves to-
> gether and made loincloths for themselves.
>
> GENESIS 3:6–7

Eve has long been used as a symbol of all that is wrong with
women: gorgeously naked, an apple in one hand, alluringly hood-
winking her husband.

For those rightfully rebelling against that depiction, Eve has
become an icon of girl power: gorgeously naked, an apple in one
hand, and in the other, the snake, a symbol of divine wisdom and
regenerative power.

I cherish reclamations of women whose stories have been weap-
onized to make us small, obedient, and fearful—particularly because Eve is so brutally blamed for the sin of all humanity. But I do
not think Eve was blameless or perfect. I think she was human.
And I want women to be seen and treated as full human beings.

We can be angry about how women have been blamed without needing to put women on a pedestal of perfection to justify our dignity. I am a woman. I am also a sinner—not because I am a woman, but because I am a human. So what does that mean, in a liberated life? How can we reclaim Eve and, at the same time, see her folly? I think we have to go back to the text, rolling away the boulders of centuries of misinterpretation, embellishment, biblical fanfiction (looking at you, *Paradise Lost*), and violent sexualization, and see what might sing to us anew.

Genesis 3:1 begins, "Now the serpent was more crafty than any other wild animal that the LORD God had made." By the way, the serpent is *not* the devil, or Satan, or any other cunning creature designed to trip people up. This snake is just a snake.

And the snake says to Eve, "Though God said, you shall not eat from any tree of the garden—" but, as biblical scholar Robert Alter emphasizes with an em dash in his translation, Eve cuts him off midsentence. "We may eat of the fruit of the trees in the garden, but God said, 'You shall not eat of the fruit of the tree that is in the middle of the garden, nor shall you touch it, or you shall die'" (Genesis 3:2–3).

This is, technically, an addition on Eve's part; God told her (and Adam, who is *right next to her when all of this is happening*) not to eat the fruit of the Tree of Knowledge, but God did *not* say, *Don't touch it*. Some scholars have posited that this is perhaps the sin: Eve adds her own words to God's law. I think Eve is just doing what all of us are left to do: interpret the words of God in our real lives.

Either way, the serpent is undaunted and continues to try to persuade her, telling her she will not be *doomed* to die, because God knows that when she eats this fruit, she will "see clearly" and *she* "*will be like God*, knowing good and evil" (Genesis 3:5, CEB, emphasis mine).

And here is where I think Eve's error lies. It is not, as I have heard in thousands of sermons and pop culture references (or as is depicted in *Paradise Lost*), in her consuming the fruit and then leading her husband down the garden path to ruin. (Remember: Adam is right next to her *the whole time*!) Nor is it in her desire for wisdom.

I think Eve's sin is her desire to be like God. Or to be "as gods," depending on the translation of verse 5. Because Eve gives the fruit a second glance after hearing the serpent's words. As Jewish scholar Robert Alter translates, Eve sees the fruit is "a lust to the eyes" and the tree is "lovely to look at." And with lust in her eyes, she makes a decision.*

Let's be clear: Lust here does not refer to her curves, or to the passion she and Adam have shared as they became one flesh, naked and unashamed. The lust Eve has is not some wanton feminine sexuality that must be policed for millennia to come by telling women that we must suffer as some eternal punishment for a figurehead who dared to ask questions.

No. The lust in Eve's eyes was a craving to be like God.

Eve had everything she could want: her lover, the Garden, their home, enough food to eat, and purposeful work (naming and caring for all animals and creation). And she decided she wanted *more*: to be like God.

---

* Incidentally, Adam makes the exact same decision without any of the theological debate Eve engaged in with the snake. She, at least, is willing to consider her choices; Adam seems more thoughtless about it and will later blame Eve for his choices and God for making Eve, so he's not exactly a moral paragon, either.

It feels almost impossible to peel the layers back on this craving to be Godlike *without* demonizing Eve for being a woman who wanted to have it all. I do not fault any woman for wanting more. I mean, my God, I'm writing this book on top of being a full-time priest, a full-time wife, and a full-time mother. I never "have it all"—or at least, never all at once. I'm always hungering for the disparate parts of my life to coagulate together so I don't feel guilty for working when I am mothering, or mothering when I am working, and so on and so forth.

But also? I do not live in a lush garden where my food is provided for me out of the abundance of a good God without my needing to work for a paycheck. I mean, my food *is* provided by a good God, but I don't get to laze about eating pomegranate seeds and delighting in the nuptial bower day in and day out without worrying about a mortgage payment.

But Eve and Adam did. And they together decided: it would be good to be like God. It would be good, better even, to take what was not theirs, to have Godlike power.

Every dictator who has ever ruled wanted Godlike power. The temptation to abuse other people, especially when we have been abused ourselves, is rooted in a desire to be like God. The temptation to force our will on other people, the temptation to take what is not ours, and especially the temptation to build structures and systems that allow us to steal from others while asserting we *deserve it* and they do not—this behavior is rooted in a desire to be like God. To have the capacity to overwrite someone else's free will and inscribe it with our own. I said earlier that we were not born in sin, we were born homesick, born in our human limitations. That does not mean sin is not real; it means trying to overcome our limitations to be like God is a sin.

But God actually gives us free will, which is exactly what Eve and Adam utilize in what we know comes next: Eve and Adam eat this fruit and—spoiler alert—they do not become gods. They become acutely aware of just how human, and vulnerable, and naked they are. And this knowledge, one we all grow into, is terrible to bear. To know we are not God, to know we can never control what happens to us or the ones we love—at least, not fully—is terrifying.

But God does not abandon them in their newfound, illicitly gained knowledge. Eve and Adam face consequences, but the consequences are not eternal damnation, nor are the two obliterated from the story of God and God's people. To paraphrase my friend and colleague Fr. Patrick Cheng, this story—and how we think about sin and God's response to sin in general—is about a lot more than crime and punishment. Notice: the "punishment" (or even the "acquittal") for this is God wrapping us in grace. God literally makes clothes for Eve and Adam. It's such an easy detail to skip over, but God stops and stitches something better for them to wear than their hastily sewn fig leaves. Grace wraps around our foolishness, and our cruelty, and whispers: *There is more here than fear, there is more to be had than domination, there is more God than human folly.* As my friend Candice Marie Benbow says, "Grace doesn't blind us to who we have been—or shield us from taking accountability for the pain we cause—but it provides us with second, third, fourth, and hundredth chances to become better people."

And that is why it is actually a grace to me that Eve's is a story about sin. The millennia of misogyny aside (ahem), God is still God, and God is still with us in the gardens (and plains and valleys and mountaintops) of our lives. God did not make us to hold the terrible burden of all knowledge, and when terrible knowledge does haunt us, God has not abandoned us to the snake in our ear whispering we are unworthy and unwanted.

God is enough God for us.

. . . .

Creator of the stars at night,
     You are the source of life and the fulfillment of
          our lives;
     heal us from our hunger for endless more.

Help us be sated with what You have given us to be
          ours.
     Help us trust You are the planter of every fruit
          tree,
     the keeper of all knowledge.

When we feel afraid of how human we are,
          comfort us.
     When we are tempted to seize what is not ours,
          stay us.
     When we long for more, remind us of Your
          abundance.

With Your Spirit that kisses our curiosity
          and Your Son who knows the meaning of
               hunger,
          one God who always has been and always will
               be:
     Amen.

7

Who Told You That You Are Naked?

· · · · · · · · · · · · · · · ·

The Lord God called to the man and said to him,
"Where are you?" The man replied, "I heard your
sound in the garden; I was afraid because I was naked, and I hid myself." He said, "Who told you that
you were naked?"

GENESIS 3:9–11 (CEB)

I do not remember ever being unashamed of my body, but I remember one of the moments when that shame was born in it.

I was maybe seven or eight, and on vacation with my extended
family on the coast. We were waiting for a table in a restaurant,
and a man approached me. I don't remember what he said, just that
it was flattering. I liked his attention. He also felt vaguely sinister
in a way I couldn't name, but I was raised to be polite, so polite I
was. And I was raised by adoring parents who laughed when I
twirled and talked, so I twirled and talked to this man. And he
laughed. And he was backing, ever so slowly, toward his boat an-
chored by the dock. And I, threaded into his web, was ever so
slowly following him.

Until my father and uncle saw what was happening.

I don't remember exactly what they said, but they were terri-fying. Furious. They yelled at this man to *back the f— off.* I had seen my father angry, but this—this unmoored me.

And I felt a terrible, burning sense of responsibility. Of fear. Of self-loathing.

With wild eyes, my father grasped me by the shoulders. "If he had asked you to go on his boat, would you have said yes?!"

I remember the red creep of shame in my cheeks and how I cut my hair later that summer because I didn't want to be looked at that way ever again—the way I was looked at by that predator, but also the way I was looked at by my father, who was in that mo-ment doing exactly what I would do now as a parent: panic, defend his child, and ask questions later.

I did not need to feel that shame. Little girls are not responsible for grown men's actions. My body was not the problem. My curi-osity was not the problem. A serpent had tricked me, and I didn't realize it, not because I was stupid or cruel or poorly raised but because I was a child. I wanted to be liked. I wanted to give him a positive perception of me without understanding the true nature of his perception of me.

I had been seen in my nakedness—not literally, but figuratively. This man had seen my innocence and simple desire to be wanted, and he had tried to exploit it. The knowledge of my nakedness was a death to me that day.

Knowledge of nakedness is the original death, in a way. Con-sider: after Eve and Adam eat the fruit—the fruit that gives them knowledge they think will make them like God—the *first* thing they do is cover up their bodies. The first thing they do with all their newfound, Godlike knowledge is not name the animals (they've already done that) or explore the Garden's wild depths (already done that) or even cling to each other in passion (already done that). No, with their new knowledge, they cover themselves up. And when they hear God coming in the cool evening breeze, Adam hides and says he hid himself because he knew he was naked.

Eve and Adam's first experience of knowledge is shame.

They feel shame that they are naked—but God knew they were naked the whole time and never *once* told them to feel shame. To cover their nakedness. God made the warm sun and the pliant grass so they could enjoy the good gifts of their bodies as God made them: naked and unashamed.

I never really understood that phrase, "naked and unashamed," until I was bathing my newborn daughter with my husband, all of us in the tub together. My daughter was six months old or so, giggling and thrashing in the bath with complete unawareness of how exposed she was. I looked with love at her and my husband, laughing with delight at her totally unashamed shine, and I burst out with: "She's still in the Garden!"

As I write this, my daughter does not yet have knowledge of nakedness. Of shame. She has not yet faced the serpents of this world who will tempt her into thinking it would be good to be like God. She may want to be God in the sense that she does not want to go to bed when we tell her she must, but her folly in this is not shame—it is the condition of being a baby held in the arms of parents who *do* have the knowledge of what is safest for her. For now, at least.

And one of the terrible knowledges I bear is the knowledge that her time in the Garden is limited. Maybe God warned Eve and Adam away from the Tree of Knowledge not because God wanted to deny humans knowledge forever but because, like all parents, God wanted to wait until we earth-creatures were ready. Ready for our innocence to be transformed into maturity instead of being stolen by our desire to be gods or by the serpents who want us under their bellies.

Eve and Adam grasped for that knowledge because they thought it was simply an object, and objects are things we can manipulate. Control. Possess. But perhaps God intended for knowledge to be not a possession but a gift. Because this is how oppressive systems work: treating knowledge like an object for only a few chosen people to possess. When we are hungry for power or fame or security, we stop thinking of knowledge as a gift that invites us all into common life and start trying to seize it as an object meant for us and us alone.

But here is the good news: The Fall is in the first three chapters of the Bible. The rest of the story is what comes next. And it's a damn good story. There are lots of stories about faithful people who mistakenly try to grasp, control, and claim the gifts of God as objects or weapons, but there are also lots more stories of God staying faithful.

Because while God does punish Eve and Adam for eating the fruit, the consequences God places on Eve—pain in childbirth—is also the means by which the Garden comes into the world over and over again. Because in all the ink spilled about original sin being linked to sex, or women, or childbirth, no one can deny the reality that children are born unashamed of their nakedness. We are born without knowledge. We are born in the Garden. And that is a gift from God.

. . . .

O God who made us,
    naked and shining,

plant in our hearts a garden
where fruits and flowers bloom, unashamed,
and where we can trust You to see
    every blemish,
and every scar,
and still say: *You, beloved, are mine.*
In the name of Christ, who took on human
    flesh,
who with You and the Spirit breathes life anew
    into us,
be all glory, honor, and praise to You, one God,
in glory everlasting.
Amen.

PART II

Redeeming the Bible

MYTH: The Bible is a cut-and-dried rulebook that is directly applicable to my twenty-first-century life, regardless of historical context or intertextual analysis.

MYSTERY: The Bible is a collection of holy stories, laws, struggles, and letters that have withstood millennia and invite us into a greater story with God.

The Holy Bible is not, it turns out, a jar of mayonnaise.

It is not full of whiteness, nor is it a condiment one can simply apply to one's life without much ado. It's not that the Bible is unclear (it can be very clear) or that spending time in the scriptures will never lead to revelations about our modern life (it often does). It's just that to think we can casually flip open an at-youngest two-thousand-year-old text and find simple, tidy lessons is bizarre. The text itself can be bizarre—in a good, if complex, way.

The Bible lives in this weird space between literature, poetry, and prayer. It is a living story that anyone, whether or not they have fancy degrees, can encounter meaning within. Most of human history with the Bible is made up of illiterate people hearing the stories proclaimed and, through these stories, connecting with the greater story of God. It is only very recently in the history of human beings and the history of the Bible that more than a handful of people can read, let alone do interlinear biblical analysis with the help of a computer we keep in our pockets. So it's kind of inevitable, I think, that there are some big bumps along the way as we all encounter an unsubdued, holy story in this new way.

As Ecclesiastes 1:9 says, there is nothing new under the sun, and that includes willful and/or ignorant misinterpretation of scripture. So to unpack the myths around what the Bible says, I think we need to dive into the mystery that a book—a book!—is one way we hear the Word that sets us free.

Scripture is not a literal rulebook, though the Law (also known as Torah, or the Laws given by God in the first five books of the Bible) is a part of scripture. But even those who keep the Law know it is more than a list of rules—it is a library of ancient, wild love stories between people and God.

The Bible is a long, winding love story. And we get to receive these holy stories and the resonances they offer in the same way we behold stained glass: we can see the light of God coming through the window of the story, and we see, feel, and experience the beautiful interplay between the two.

8

Sarah Laughed at God,
and God Liked It

....

Now Abraham and Sarah were old, advanced in age. . . . So Sarah laughed to herself, saying, "After I have grown old, and my husband is old, shall I be fruitful?"

GENESIS 18:11–12

Margaret Atwood once wrote that men are afraid women will laugh at them, while women are afraid men will kill them. Of course, *no one* wants to be laughed at. But the contrast between a fear of men being violent and a fear of women laughing says a lot about what we as a society feel threatened by. We don't worry so much about women causing physical harm; rather, we see their greatest weapon as the capacity for *laughter*.

Which might be why Sarah's laughter in Genesis has often been portrayed with such disdain.

Abraham and Sarah are a married couple whose story spans some forty chapters in the book of Genesis, the first book of the Bible. They are called by God to leave their homeland, at great peril, and settle in a new place where God will guide them. For being such famous biblical figures, Abraham and Sarah have a *very* morally gray story. They are not always kind, or faithful, or loving. Yet, for whatever reason, God has chosen them to make a promise: that Abraham's descendants will be so many, they will be more numerous than the stars in the sky or the hairs on his head.

But the thing is, Abraham and Sarah go a long time without successfully conceiving and carrying a pregnancy to term. Like, a *long* time—Sarah is postmenopausal when the story we'll explore in this devotion picks up. During this long wait for a child, they often lose faith, and their lack of faith leads to brutal consequences (including the exploitation of people in their household, which I'll discuss in the next devotion).

But God persists, and in Genesis 18, angels visit Abraham. Understandably, Abraham flies into a panic. He knows these are divine guests, so he shoos Sarah out of the way, telling her to mix up three measures of flour into bread. (For reference, that is *sixty pounds* of flour. It is an unhinged amount of food.) Sarah—dutifully, or grumbling, or both—stands in the tent, kneading this dough. And she overhears the angels say, *The next time we visit, Sarah will have a son.*

And, tucked out of sight of the menfolk, maybe dealing with a hot flash of menopause as she's making an obscenely large amount of food, Sarah *laughs*. And to herself she asks: "Will I now have this pleasure?" (Genesis 18:12, NIV).

Which: fair enough. God has made promise after promise about children, and still, no baby for Sarah. She is old. Could God, who has drawn her and Abraham away from home, led them through terrible trials, whose promises have started to taste like dust, really give her the *pleasure* of motherhood? After all these years of anxiety, of loss, of longing?

So Sarah *laughs*. Maybe it is a laugh of incredulity. Maybe it is a snort of derisive disbelief. Maybe it is the rip-roaring guffaw of a woman who knows if she doesn't laugh, she'll cry. But she laughs. She laughs at God! And God overhears Sarah laughing, and God even brings it up to Abraham: "Why did Sarah laugh and say, 'Shall I indeed bear a child, now that I am old?' Is anything too wonderful for the LORD?" (Genesis 18:13–14). To which Sarah, in a panic, insists she did not laugh. To which God insists: *Oh yes, you did!*

I have heard a lot of poor imagination around this story. Some people ask how Sarah could dare to laugh at God, or use God's response as proof God was mad that Sarah would make a mockery of Him. There's a lot of talk about how we shouldn't disrespect our Heavenly Father, lest He chastise us the way He chastises Sarah here.

But is that response about God? Or is it about what we incorrectly call "God"? Because God does not punish Sarah. God *does* give Sarah this pleasure. Because God does not share the fear of laughter Margaret Atwood named. To say God is mad at Sarah for laughing disregards that God is standing *with* Sarah in the kitchen. Sarah is not in the important meeting between Abraham and the angels out front—she's talking to herself while rolling out the dough—but God hears her. We know this for sure because God even mentions it to Abraham in the middle of his important meeting away from the domesticity of the kitchen.

That the Lord hears Sarah's laughter, away from the men's main-character action, tells me that God cares about the places where people are sent to be outside of the proverbial room where it happens. God cares about the people in the kitchen, eavesdropping to overhear. And when Sarah laughs at the ridiculousness of the idea that she, a postmenopausal woman, would bear a child,

God doesn't shame or silence Sarah. God asks, *Is* anything *too marvelous for the Lord?*

Contrary to a patriarchal response in which masculine power is threatened by feminine laughter, God is the all-powerful anti-patriarch who says: *Yes, you did laugh, and no, nothing is too marvelous for God.* Not even the exhilarated, doubtful, wild laughter of an old woman being promised she would do something new.

How often in our own lives do we assume something is too marvelous for the Lord? Sometimes we do this the way Sarah did, when beautiful, absurd, good things are spoken over us, before us, in us, and we say, *No, no way.*

And you know what the real rub is? When we believe or act like God is a bully who punishes our laughter, we are trying to make God smaller. We underestimate God by assuming God doesn't want our joy, our giggles, our incredulity. We think a life of faith must always be serious, with no room for laughter (especially from behind the main action, back in the kitchen).

I mean, do we really think the dreamer-upper of the seahorse or the aurora borealis is a boring, stodgy old man? What would our faith look like if, instead of thinking of God as a solemn and unapproachable power, we instead imagined . . . more? A Father who laughs *with* His children, and not at them? A God who is bigger than any power we can see and therefore undaunted by our pleasure? A God who beholds a barren woman's grief and disbelief and laughter and says: *Oh, my darling, there is nothing too marvelous for me and you, together. There is nothing too marvelous for the Lord.*

. . . .

God of Delight:
    To know You is perfect freedom.*
    Help us trust that all of who we are is cherished
        by You,
    and that we can be free to laugh,
    free to trust,
    free to know You want only good things for us
        and all in this good, good world You
        knitted together.
    We pray this through Jesus Christ, Your only
        Son, our Lord,
    who lives and reigns with You and the Holy
        Spirit,
    one God in glorious joy everlasting.
    Amen.

---

* From "A Collect for Peace" in "Daily Morning Prayer: Rite Two" (Episcopal Church, *The Book of Common Prayer* [New York: Church Publishing, 1979], 99.)

9

Hagar, the Enslaved Woman Who Named God

. . . .

So Hagar named the Living God who spoke to her:
"You are El-ro'i"; for she said, "Have I really seen
God and remained alive after seeing God?"

GENESIS 16:13
(TRANSLATED BY REV. WILDA C. GAFNEY)

I imagine her caked with dust from the road, nauseous from the running and first-trimester sickness. Her body still aches from where her mistress beat her, mercilessly, for doing exactly what she had been told to do. And now she has taken fate into her own hands and run away.

She comes upon a spring of water. She is taking that first blessed sip when the stranger interrupts her: "Hagar, slave of Sarai, where have you come from and where are you going?" (Genesis 16:8).

And Hagar replies, "I am running away from my mistress Sarai" (Genesis 16:8).

As I mentioned in the last devotion, Sarai—who will become Sarah—had grown impatient waiting for the child God kept promising her. So she foisted her husband upon her Egyptian enslaved woman and said, *Here. Have a surrogate.* This was not an uncommon thing for enslavers to do to the women they enslaved, but that does not change the fact that Hagar would have had little to no ability to say no. Hagar conceived. And instead of joyfully preparing for the coming baby, Sarai became bitter that she wasn't the one having the child—and then she became violent with Hagar.

So Hagar ran. Risking her life and the life of her unborn child, she escaped into the desert, where we now meet her stopped for water at a spring. And at the spring, she is approached by an angel, a messenger, of the Lord. And that angel tells her to "return . . . and submit to" Sarai, despite the abuse (Genesis 16:9).

This is undoubtedly the last thing Hagar wants to hear in this moment. But then the message pivots. The messenger uses words that directly parallel the promise that just a few chapters earlier God had given to Hagar's enslaver and father of her child, Abraham. And the messenger of God promises that Hagar's seed will be multiplied such that it cannot be counted. A name is given to her unborn son: Ishmael, meaning "God hears." As womanist biblical scholar Wilda Gafney notes, not only is Hagar the first woman in scripture granted an annunciation (a foretelling of birth from God), but also *she* gets credit for *her own* offspring. This is wildly unusual; credit for offspring is language that is usually reserved for men in the Bible.

There is a paradox here of tremendous promise and pain. On the one hand, God is telling Hagar to go back to a situation where she has endured physical and sexual abuse. On the other hand, God is promising a legacy to Hagar that is not promised to any other woman, including Sarai.

How did Hagar respond to this paradox? "She named the LORD who spoke to her, 'You are El-ro'i'"—Hebrew for "the God who sees" or "the God who is seen"—"for she said, 'Have I really seen God and remained alive after seeing him?'" (Genesis 16:13).

While many people in the Bible ascribe titles to God or invoke the help of God by calling upon God's characteristics, Hagar is the only person to *name* God. As biblical scholar Phyllis Trible notes, in the original Hebrew syntax, others *call upon* the name of God, but Hagar *calls* the name of God, which is "a power attributed to no one else in all the Bible." The only person to *give* God a name in the whole Bible is an African enslaved pregnant woman who is running away from the brutal torment of her enslavers.

And, as womanist biblical scholar Delores Williams notes, Hagar does not name God with the same kinds of words she has heard Sarai and Abram use to describe God, like "Lord" or "Master." Instead of using the language of mastery and enslavement, Hagar names God out of her own faith and understanding as "the God Who Sees/Is Seen." Williams wonders, "Was Hagar's naming of God an act of defiance and resistance as well as an expression of awe?" Can faith be both defiant and awe-filled? Can faith claim that God was with us through the bad things and that God's ways are not ours to grasp, while also asserting that we are as beloved by God as any person who harms us?

Yes. Hagar's faith can. Her faith shows us we can, too.

We can know God may ask us to endure some very un-Godlike treatment, while also knowing God will make a way out of no way. Because Hagar trusts God enough to obey, to turn around and walk back into a terrible situation. And yet so much of Christian history has not valued the story of Hagar as one of faithful obedience to God in terrible times. She is often overlooked in favor of the "heroes of the faith" who enslaved her, Sarah and Abraham.

And then in the 1990s, the aforementioned Delores Williams

found Hagar's story to be so generative she wrote a book called *Sisters in the Wilderness*, and this incredible book gave birth to the flourishing discipline of womanist biblical studies*—that is, reading the Bible in the context of Black women's flourishing. Writer Alice Walker defined "womanist" not just as "a black feminist or feminist of color" but also as "a woman who loves other women, sexually and/or nonsexually," someone with "outrageous, audacious, courageous or willful behavior" who "Loves music. Loves dance. Loves the moon. Loves the Spirit"—and so much more. Applying these ideas to the study of the Bible, Williams breathed new life into how we read about Hagar and her complex, audacious, defiant faith in a God who sees her.

I want to be clear: I am a guest in womanist conversations, not an expert. But it would be an anemic devotional indeed if I did not include Hagar, and if I wrote about Hagar without mentioning the brilliant work womanist scholars have done to illuminate her story. Redeeming the Bible from the damage of white supremacy is collaborative work. I think the best of Christian conversation means we all learn from people whose experiences are radically different from our own, but who all know and love the same God.

Womanism has taught me, as a white woman, that to read scripture with liberating hope demands we read ourselves into the story both in the fringes (Hagar) and in the villains (Sarah and Abraham, in this story), and that we see both the fringe and the villains as people in the wholeness of the story of God.

I do not relish thinking of myself as a villain. But I am stuck in

---

* An abbreviated list of scholars I am indebted to: Wilda C. Gafney, Renita J. Weems, Eboni Marshall Turman, Kelly Brown Douglas, Katie G. Cannon, Emilie M. Townes, Monica A. Coleman, and Jacquelyn Grant.

the sin of self-deception if I think I never have been a villain. Even the arguments that say I benefit from white privilege are a bit tepid: racism is in the water in America. (I mean that metaphorically, but also literally: look at Flint, Michigan.) Of *course* I have benefited from racism, knowingly and unknowingly, and just as I confess my sins every day, I must work every day to uproot this sinfulness from within me.

And this, too, is what Hagar names when she says, "You are the God who sees." God sees us in our public and private moments. God sees all of us, for all of who we are, including the parts we don't even want to reveal to ourselves.

But perhaps more important to name: God sees when you are overlooked, harmed, and neglected because of how the world values or does not value you. God sees you when you feel so alone, so isolated, so terrified that you're not sure if you can take another step.

God is big enough, and holy enough, to love Hagar, and to love Sarah and Abraham. God sees the long arc of our lives, and the long arc of the universe, and God may send us where we desperately do not want to go, but God will never send us where God is not with us.

And God sees. God sees the invisible burden, the crushing loneliness, the double-speak. God sees. And God will not forsake you.

. . . .

El-ro'i, God who sees:
  there are things we bury and hide,
  things that corrode our souls with their
      violence,
  things of which we are ashamed to speak.

Help us trust: You see, and still, You love.
    Help us trust: You will never, ever send us
        anywhere alone.
    Help us know: when there is no way, Your way
        will make a way.

Jesus, You have never failed us.
    Spirit, Your sweetness is here on the bitterest
        day.
    Mother, You will not let us stray.

Guide us, hold us, carry us home.

Amen.

· 10 ·

Joseph's Fabulous Couture Coat

....

Then they said to one another, "Look, this dreamer
is coming! Come therefore, let us now kill him and
cast him into some pit; and we shall say, 'Some
wild beast has devoured him.' We shall see what
will become of his dreams!"

GENESIS 37:19–20 (NKJV)

Joseph the Dreamer is a biblical character most famous for his coat.
And, legit, it was a *very* fabulous coat. This coat was of many colors, and it was ornamented, ornate, with long flamboyant sleeves.
Jacob, Joseph's dad, gave him this coat to show all the world (and
his other eleven sons) that Joseph was his most, most favorite.

Such a garment was expensive. In the words of biblical scholar
Robert Alter, it "was a product of ancient haute couture," which we
know not only because of Joseph's story but also because the
words used to describe Joseph's coat in Genesis 37 are the exact
same words used in 2 Samuel to describe the clothing worn by
Tamar, the daughter of King David (who, like Joseph, faces a violent act of betrayal by a sibling). While clothes do not dictate gender or sexuality, they certainly are vehicles of gender and sexual

expression, so I think it's important we pay attention to the fact that Joseph is wearing a princess robe. (I mean, not literally, but you get my drift.)*

If Joseph were not already a queer icon in the Bible for his couture coat of many colors, what happens to him has unmistakable parallels to anti-queer violence today. Joseph wasn't just Daddy's favorite—he also was blessed by God (ugh, so spoiled) with prophetic dreams. In these dreams, he saw his eleven brothers bowing before him. Over and over. And (like an absolute brat) Joseph tells his eleven brothers all about these dreams.

This goes about as well as you might think it would.

Joseph's brothers are, understandably, jealous of him. While they're toiling in the fields and tending the flocks, Joseph is hanging out with Dad in the tent, lounging about in a princess robe. And out there in those fields, they begin to plot how to handle this self-obsessed, bratty little brother of theirs. Boiling over with jealousy, the brothers hatch a plot to kill Joseph.

Unaware of this resentment, their father sends Joseph out to check on his brothers. The brothers see Joseph cresting the hill in the distance, no doubt coming to spy and tattle to their father. And so they turn to each other and say, *Here comes the dreamer. Let's kill him, and then we'll see what becomes of those dreams of his.* This is the clarion call of fear underneath every hate crime: *This person has dreams. This person sees a world that I cannot fathom. They can imagine in full Technicolor, and that scares me.*

Because, to be super clear: it may not be fair that Joseph is the favorite, but he does not deserve what is about to happen to him.

---

* Alter makes the case that this was a "unisex" garment; even so, this shows gender expression has never been a monolith.

The brothers pivot from their murder plan when they realize they can make a profit off of his demise by trafficking him into slavery. So when Joseph arrives, they violently rip off his beloved coat of many colors, smear it with blood, and lie to their father that he was eaten by a wild animal, when in reality they have sold him to slave traders for twenty pieces of silver.

I see this scene so vividly in my mind, and it is colored with the lament of Matthew Shepard, a young gay man who was brutally tortured by two men in his community in Laramie, Wyoming, in 1998, and died of his injuries. I see Akira Ross, a young Black gay woman who was murdered *across the street from my church* in Texas by a man who called her an anti-gay slur before shooting her in 2023. I see trans women who are attacked for simply existing. I see the echoes of child abuse in the terror Joseph must have felt as his *siblings* did this to him; surely, he begged them to stop.

"Behold, here cometh the dreamer . . . let us slay him . . . and we shall see what will become of his dreams." This rendition of Genesis 37:19–20 is emblazoned in stone underneath the balcony of the Lorraine Motel in Memphis, Tennessee. Because it was on that balcony, in April 1968, that Martin Luther King Jr., a dreamer, was assassinated by white supremacist powers who did not want his dreams to keep catching on.

Evil is afraid to dream in color, every color. Evil is afraid of freedom. As queer trans activist Alok Vaid-Menon says:

> The resentment and bitterness that people have toward me and my community—and when I say "my community," I don't just mean trans people, I mean people living their own lives—is because they're looking at us saying, "What do

you mean that we get to be free?" People use their suffering as an emblem of their worth: I had to clip my wings, so you must, too. I'm sorry you had to go through that, but that doesn't give you license to make *other* people have to go through that. So the advice I would give to people is that it is possible to be alive but be spiritually dead.

Vaid-Menon tells it like it is: *hatred is a spiritual death*. If we were made to be free, then living in cages of our own making—for ourselves and for others—is antithetical to what God wants for us.

I wonder if you resonate with Joseph and the violence he faced. I wonder if you resonate with the brothers and their envy, their fear. If I'm honest, I can resonate with both—not the doing of a hate crime, but the envy that was its seed. I have been both: the oppressor and the oppressed. I have been terrified to live out loud, have made myself smaller to make myself less of a threat for living in my joy. And I have been bitter, jealous, and angry when I saw other people living into a freedom I did not feel I could allow myself.

This is why resurrection matters: the temptation into spiritual death is all around us. In envy. In fear. In scapegoating whole communities of people because the world has changed and that scares us. In believing we deserve less because we are too much.

But this is a death that Christ gives us the power to resist: both as the victims in the pit and as the ones tempted to put others in the pit. Because Christ came for all of us to have *life* and to have *life abundant*.

God desires us to have glorious, flamboyant life in many colors. In every color of the rainbow.

. . . .

God who painted the rainbow,
    exceedingly beautiful in its brightness,*
    we praise You.

You covered Joseph in Your love
    as he was stripped naked and thrown into the
        pit.
    We know Your love has blanketed so many of
        our queer ancestors,
    tenderly carrying them home
    when they were taken from us, too soon.
    O God, they were taken too soon.

Help us see: You have been with us in every pit,
    counting the hairs on our heads and whispering,
        I made you to shine.

Forgive us for when we thought freedom was cheap
    enough to be sold;
    forgive us for making ourselves smaller and
        calling it Your will;
    we beg Your mercy for the harm done in Your
        holy name.

---

* Adapted from Sirach 43:11.

We beg You:
    pry wide our cages as only You can.

Show us the meaning of Your freedom, Your life,
        for all of us.
    All of us.

Amen.

· 11 ·

The Brutality of Mercy

. . . .

But Joseph said to them, ". . . You planned something bad for me, but God produced something
good from it, in order to save the lives of many
people, just as he's doing today."

GENESIS 50:19–20 (CEB)

Joseph was given dreams by God, and he was trusting enough, and
imaginative enough, to believe them. He shared these dreams
with his brothers, and his brothers threw him into a pit, tore his
beloved coat of many colors, and then sold him into slavery—for
his dreams.

Imagination is the capacity to see hope in color. And you can
identify evil, real evil, when it is afraid of imagination. Evil—the
snaking temptation that lurks around mob mentality, that incar-
cerates, that categorizes some people as worthy and others as
vile—is a force that is colorless. Imagination sees what is, and
what is good about what is, and also sees how it could be better.
The language of imagination is dreams. And evil is afraid of our
dreams. Evil is afraid of a world full of riotous color and fabulous,
ornamented outfits, afraid of the confidence we deserve to have as

children who walk knowing we are loved by our good Father in heaven who sewed every piece of us together with love.

And evil *should* be afraid of our dreams. Because God does not abandon Her children, even when people in God's name abandon us. And all those dreams God gave to Joseph? All those dreams came true. The pit that Joseph's brothers throw him into is not the end of the story. Joseph goes through many, many trials, but many years later, the dreams he had of his brothers—that they would lie prostrate before him, borderline worshipping him? That comes true.

A famine comes to the land of Canaan, where the brothers live. Faced with few options, the brothers travel to Egypt in search of grain. In a twist of divine irony, *Joseph* is the person they must beg for food. Because in the years since the pit, Joseph has worked his way up to be the Egyptian pharaoh's right-hand man—because of his dreams. Pharaoh was plagued with nightmares, and Joseph interpreted these dreams, rightly, to mean that a famine was coming. This prediction helped the Egyptians save enough food to withstand the famine. So the brothers who had plunged Joseph into the pit had no food, while Joseph was doing just fine.

Joseph's brothers don't recognize him at first. But Joseph knows exactly who they are at first sight. And initially he is furious, and hurt, and he has them imprisoned as spies for a while, driving them to panic and terror. But eventually, in an act so merciful and so loving it can only be of God, Joseph reveals himself as the brother they tried to kill, and, as the brothers prepare for his rightful retribution upon them, Joseph tells them: "Even though you intended to do harm to me, God intended it for good, in order to preserve a numerous people, as he is doing today" (Genesis 50:20).

There is no reason Joseph needs to forgive his brothers. He holds complete power over them; he could demand anything from them. They are literally *at his mercy*. He could kill them all. He could put them all in a pit and do to them exactly what they did to him. But the story seems to suggest Joseph is so overwhelmed, so awed by the power he has to *save* his family—whom he thought were lost to him forever *by their own doing*—that mercy erupts out of him.

When Joseph says, "What you intended for evil, God has used for good," it is vital we remember the person who was wronged is telling this story. The person who was harmed gets to claim where God was in that evil pit. And, to be very clear, Joseph's extension of mercy does not erase the wrong done to him, nor does it seem to come easy for him, nor does it seem to immediately ease the ache of his brothers' heavy consciences.

Mercy is brutal. It is not popular, or easy, or alluring. Mercy is so hard to give, and to receive, because mercy is hardly ever *deserved*.

But that is why mercy matters. Because there are things we do, or that have been done to us, that are bad and need redeeming. Doing something bad does not mean we are beyond redeeming, or that we are doomed to be bad forever. And mercy does not mean cosigning on what was done to us. To paraphrase my colleague Rev. Kelli Joyce, forgiveness inherently recognizes that what happened was *not okay*, because the act of forgiving inherently acknowledges that something bad has happened. We do not forgive good things. We do not forgive people who have done us no harm.

To forgive, to choose the brutal path of mercy, is to say: I am choosing more—more life, more freedom, more possibility—even in the face of something or someone who wanted to steal my freedom, steal my possibilities, and possibly even end my life. This is why mercy comes from God. Because how else could Joseph choose mercy, if not by God's grace?

But the deepest brutality of this mercy is that, no matter how much Joseph hated and was hurt by his brothers, he surely also *missed* them. Because he could have chosen to hurt them back, but then he would have had vengeance but no family. The brutality of mercy meant there was a new path, fragile but powerful, for all of them to try: the path of a second chance. The path of righting a wrong by living for now, not then.

Mercy is an act of imagination. It imagines there can be so much more—more color, more forgiveness, more joy, more time together—if we can be more than the worst things we have ever done. If we can be more than the worst things done to us. Mercy is brutal. But mercy is also beautiful. It dreams of a world where we can all be free—free from the pit and free from the burning desire to put people in the pit. Mercy is a language of God's imagination for what we can be, all of us, together.

. . . .

Holy God,
    holy and mighty,
    holy immortal One,
    have mercy on us.

Paint our imagination with Your dreams for what
    we can be, who we can be.
Give us courage to step into the unknown,
    knowing You are there.

Help us release the chains we wear as armor,
so that we can be free to know our pain
and our sutures
are part of Your tapestry
which is more colorful than eyes can see.
Amen.

12

Is It Exodus?
Or Is It Texas?

. . . .

The king of Egypt spoke to two Hebrew midwives
named Shiphrah and Puah: "When you are helping
the Hebrew women give birth and you see the baby
being born, if it's a boy, kill him. But if it's a girl,
you can let her live." Now the two midwives respected God so they didn't obey the Egyptian
king's order. Instead, they let the baby boys live.

EXODUS 1:15–17 (CEB)

A woman is weaving a basket of reeds and pitch. Weaving with
the sweet lullaby of a mother and the desperation of a woman under siege, because this basket is to be a waterproof (but not bulletproof) cradle. She is praying with every strand that her son will
be safe from the tyranny of the government that wants him dead.
He is only a baby. But she lowers him into his river bassinet and
prays that these thin walls of grass and her last lullaby will keep
him safe.

The world must be an awfully dangerous place if a river, with
its wild currents and terrifying predators, is the best option for

this mother and her child. And still, she places her baby in the water, because there is no safety left for him on land.

Is this the story of Exodus? Or is it Texas?

I live in Texas, and I have been many times to the Rio Grande, the river where many people try to cross the border into the United States. I have been in asylum-seeking camps full of people forced to live in inhumane conditions as they await an inhumane immigration process. I have seen Pharaoh's fear in the chalk drawings left by children that say "Choose love" next to their dilapidated tents, and I have been left wondering: *What are anti-immigration politicians so afraid of?*

In the story of Exodus, the government has told all the midwives, all the medical practitioners, that they are not to let Hebrew mothers keep their children. The government does not want women to have a choice. Pharaoh tries to turn healers into murderers for his own fear-based agenda. He deploys two midwives, whose names are Shiphrah and Puah, to limit the population growth of the people he has systematically exploited—because he is afraid if their numbers grow large enough, they will seek retribution for that exploitation.

Now, as womanist scholar Wilda Gafney points out, the story is not clear if Shiphrah and Puah, these "Hebrew midwives" (Exodus 1:15), are Egyptian midwives to the Hebrews, making them members of the dominant ethnic group, or if they are themselves Hebrew women, members of the oppressed outgroup. But the story is clear on this: these women betray their pharaoh. They will not harm these children, and they will not rob mothers of their choice to keep their children with them.

It would not be too anachronistic to say that these midwives embody what we would today call Reproductive Justice: a movement with ancient roots that "was developed by African American feminists in 1994 and subsequently popularized by many women of color through the leadership of the SisterSong Women of Color Reproductive Justice Collective," according to Dr. Loretta J. Ross, one of the leaders of this movement. Reproductive Justice moves beyond the binary of "choice" vs. "no choice," which does not sufficiently reflect the complex and intersecting realities that communities of Indigenous, immigrant, Black, queer, and trans people face in their reproductive lives. Rather, Reproductive Justice emphasizes the human rights of all people to have children, to not have children, and to nurture the children we have in a safe and healthy environment.

What I have learned as a person of faith from the Spiritual Alliance of Communities for Reproductive Dignity (SACReD) is that these stories of reproductive dignity are not new, but can be found right here in the Bible. And as part of my Christian call, I can "work for a world where families have the resources to flourish, and everyone is free to make decisions about their body with dignity at every stage of life." This is what Shiphrah and Puah do. It is an essential part of human dignity to be able to raise children in safety.

Is this story about Exodus? Or is this story about Texas?

As a priest, I have borne witness to miscarriage, stillbirth, and the devastating consequences of moralizing and legalizing reproductive lives like they are simplistic choices on a menu. And this story in Exodus—and Texas—ought to teach us that when hard-hearted leaders operate out of fear, they are dealing in death, not life.

The mother whose birth was protected by Shiphrah and Puah puts her baby in a basket to float a river that could be the Rio

Grande or the Nile. The baby's sister watches from a distance; perhaps she was the only one in the family who could stomach it, the curiosity of a child insulating her from the fears carried by the grown-ups in her life. And she watches as her baby brother is tossed about, avoiding crocodile teeth and other dangers, until he lands safely in the bathing spot of a wealthy woman. A powerful, wealthy woman—the daughter of the very pharaoh who ordered this baby be killed.

What does she do? Does she turn this innocent, no doubt squalling child over to her father? Or does something unlock within her in her palace of isolation as she beholds her enemy with newborn fingers and a gummy mouth? Or is it only when this baby boy's sister—Miriam—approaches her and offers to find a wet nurse that she makes her decision?

Pharaoh's daughter can and does piece this situation together; she says, "This must be one of the Hebrews' children" (Exodus 2:6). A baby who doesn't look Egyptian followed by a little girl who doesn't look Egyptian, offering to conveniently find a nursing mother for a not-weaned child who just appeared in Pharaoh's palace bathing pool? It's too obvious, isn't it, that this is a family desperate to escape the very rule of law Pharaoh dictates?

And Pharaoh's daughter says *yes*. She says yes to a poor little girl, the daughter of an enslaved people, and she keeps the baby and names him Moses. And Miriam offers her and Moses's mother as a wet nurse. And Moses's mother gets to hold her baby, whole and healthy, for a little while longer, even though she has to watch him grow up being told a lie about whose boy he really is.

Whether it is Exodus or whether it is Texas, remember: the will of God is always greater than the empires of man. This story is just the first chapter of the Bible's best epic, and it is a story of women choosing solidarity over wealth or security. Whether it is Exodus or Texas, remember: children and their caregivers who have to cross dangerous rivers seeking safety are blessed by God, who also was an infant refugee and immigrant. Whether it is Exodus or Texas, remember: God has a long memory, and it is not Pharaoh whom God protects from the storms that are to come. God will hear the groans of the enslaved people in Egypt. And in the meantime, it is on us to be the sisterhood who seeks God in the river.

. . . .

Our help is in the Name of the Lord:
    the weaver of heaven and earth.
    She has not given us over to be prey for their
        teeth.
    Blessed be the Lord!
    By Her will we escape like a bird from the snare
        of the fowler;
    the snare is broken, and we will escape.
    She will not harden Her heart to our cries,
    She will redeem the river.

Because our help is in the Name of the Lord,
the maker of heaven and earth.[*]

Amen.

---

[*] Adapted from Psalm 124.

13

Jubilee:
God's Justice Is God's Joy

....

You will make the fiftieth year holy, proclaiming
freedom throughout the land to all its inhabitants.
It will be a Jubilee year.

LEVITICUS 25:10 (CEB)

When my fellow Christians say they take the Bible literally, I remain ever hopeful that they do in fact mean they take Leviticus
literally. Let me explain. As much ink as has been spilled over Leviticus purportedly forbidding same-sex relationships, the reality
is that far more of this book is concerned with the Law of God
being about justice and joy for all—in the release of debt, the free-
ing of captives, the feeding of the hungry, and the care of land that
is never actually ours to own.

The most scandalous, the most radical, and the most liberating
commandment God gives in the Law is found in Leviticus 25: the
commandment to observe the Jubilee Year. The year of Jubilee is
kind of a super sabbath year—and a sabbath year, which is observed every seven years (like the sabbath day is observed every
seven days), is a year of "complete rest for the land," when the peo-

ple can eat what the land naturally produces but cannot plant anything specifically to be harvested (Leviticus 25:4).

To be perfectly honest, when I first encountered the concept of a sabbath year, I didn't recognize it as much of a hardship, because I don't plant my own food. This is true of most (but certainly not all) of us, even the plant daddies and devoted gardeners. We live in a culture and time in which we are unnaturally separated from the production of our own sustenance. The backbreaking work of growing and nurturing and harvesting vegetables is largely relegated to immigrants who are subject to the whims of political tyrants; the conditions in which fish and poultry and cattle are slaughtered are cleanly wiped away with crisp plastic packaging in the aisles of the local grocery store. (My brother is a diesel mechanic, and he is haunted by the things he saw fixing equipment for poultry farms in rural North Carolina.)

But in the ancient world where these promises were first offered, all of life was oriented around . . . life. Around the planting and tending of the harvest, through which households grew their own food, both to eat and to barter for what they didn't have. To follow a commandment from God *not* to bring in a harvest is an incredibly vulnerable action.

But God does not stop with a sabbath year. Because every seven sabbath years—so every fiftieth year—there is to be a year of Jubilee. And Jubilee is a year when not only are we not to plant any food, but also we are to *completely* live off of an extravagant harvest that God promises will last for three years until we have produce again. And this isn't all: the year of Jubilee is the year that every debt is released, enslaved people are set free, and those who are food secure are commanded to seek out anyone who does not have enough to eat and feed them. In the Jubilee framework, if someone owes you money for a car payment, a college loan, a medical procedure, or anything else, every forty-nine years, it becomes completely void.

The logic of Jubilee also means that we never, ever own land—because the land is God's, and we are forever "sojourning settlers," as Jewish scholar Robert Alter translates. Land is not a possession, but a commonly held home made by God for us to dwell on.

Jubilee is a wild vision of holy justice. And in nearly every study Bible and commentary on Leviticus 25, there is this footnote along these lines: *There is no evidence any community followed the Jubilee law.*

It strikes me that part of the reason why this may be is that Jubilee can feel like an overwhelming concept when we only look at the dimensions of justice within it. How, exactly, will we ensure that every person is fed? How will we make sure every person is housed? But also, imagine with me: What would our world look like if we *did* embody Jubilee? What would your life look like if the potentially hundreds of thousands of dollars you might owe in student loans, medical bills, or mortgage payments were just . . . gone? What would it look like if everyone who owed us money was suddenly and irrevocably freed from that debt?

It is wonderful and terrifying to imagine that kind of vulnerability and interdependence on God and one another. Because if we embodied Jubilee, I suspect our world would look a lot more like God's original intention—like a resplendent, lush Garden of Eden.

God made us for *joy*. God's delight, God's profligate, excessive, gaudy, ridiculous, extravagant plan for human beings was for us to feast in a garden without shame or stigma. To simply be, together. To trust the freedom and delight that comes from this connectedness. Jubilee is about justice, and it is about God's joy. Justice and joy, for God, are so intertwined they cannot be separated.

....

Garden-keeper:
>   You know every germinating seed and aging
>   oak,
>   and You have called them all *good*.
>   Empower us to seek Your justice by knowing
>   Your joy;
>   embolden us to stay gentlehearted
>   and help us trust
>   Your harvest is enough.
>   Amen.

14

The Spiritual Discipline of Joy

....

Then he said to them, "Go your way, eat the fat and drink sweet wine and send portions of them to those for whom nothing is prepared, for this day is holy to our LORD, and do not be grieved, for the joy of the LORD is your strength."

NEHEMIAH 8:10

In her book *Dare to Lead*, Brené Brown says that "joy is the most vulnerable emotion we feel." Joy is more vulnerable than pain, than embarrassment, than shame. Joy is so incredibly vulnerable because "it's beauty and fragility and deep gratitude and impermanence all wrapped up in one experience." As Brown writes, we fear that this precious thing will be taken from us. We fear that we aren't worthy of the precious gift.

Because joy? Joy is a beckoner. True joy is effusive. It is not rooted in material gain or rancorous victory in putting someone else down. It is not happiness at the expense of someone else's loss. Joy is not concerned about being reserved only for the "in crowd." It doesn't sequester itself along neat categorical lines. Joy begets joy. And I think that's why joy is so vulnerable: because joy is the tender underbelly of our connection.

And we are living in a time when the precarity of joy is terrifying. Life is fleeting. We have not yet fully processed—and cannot yet fully process—the carnage of a global pandemic that claimed so many lives and rewrote all of our ways of living. We spent two years (plus) not trusting each other's presence for our own safety and the safety of the vulnerable. That mistrust lingers.

If you're encountering this devotional, you've likely had your own story of loss and upheaval in your faith. The ways a faith upheaval—or deconstruction, or liberation—can make us feel like an anchorless boat set adrift really cannot be overstated. Disillusion can set us free, but that freedom can feel like a free fall into . . . what? What comes next?

Never has it seemed like the time is riper to give up on hope and give in to cynicism. Between climate disaster, brutally partisan politics, horrific warfare, sexual violence, and all the everyday-but-no-less-brutal-for-it losses and diagnoses and pain, what is the *point* of joy? Isn't it just selfish when there is so much suffering? This world has proven itself over and over to be a bleak and violent place to plant a garden.

But, beloved babe of God, do not be afraid. Jesus tells us it is God's good pleasure, God's *joy*, to give us the kin-dom of God's kingdom. God gave us joy exactly *because* the world feels scary and sad and lonely. We are desperate to be interconnected. We are not made for anger and isolation and fear; we are made for this tender, gentle, joy-full connection to God and one another. And this connection is a precious thing, but it is not fragile. This world tried to kill God, and God sauntered right out of the grave and said: *Not today, Satan.* (Like, literally!)

Joy is our resilience. Joy is why we stay alive. Joy is why we believe. Joy is what waits for us when we rest. So joy is precious, and joy is resilient, and as vulnerable as it feels, we do not have to manufacture our own joy, because it is the joy of the Lord that shall be our strength (Nehemiah 8:10).

As much as we can make and partake in joy, I think the deepest truth is that joy is a spiritual discipline. Joy is most important to cherish, cultivate, and nourish when we most feel like we do not deserve joy or there is no joy to be found.

In my Episcopal tradition, we have a simple prayer service we can say at night called Compline, which has my most favorite prayer:

> Keep watch, dear Lord,
> with those who work, or watch,
> or weep this night,
> and give your angels charge over those who sleep.
> Tend the sick, Lord Christ;
> give rest to the weary,
> bless the dying,
> soothe the suffering,
> pity the afflicted,
> shield the joyous;
> and all for your love's sake.
> *Amen.*

Notice that in this prayer, in the midst of the litany of losses we intercede for—asking God to give rest to the weary and pity the afflicted—we also ask God to *shield the joyous*. This is how we practice joy as a spiritual discipline. We allow joy in, and we nourish joy when it arrives, and we pray that God will shield it—but we must not armor it. Nourish your joy not by keeping it secret or building walls around it, but by choosing joy even and especially when you feel like you don't deserve it. Choose joy when the world wants to see your happiness as empty, consumerist, and cheap. Choose joy when the connection may be fragile. Joy is still worthwhile.

And because we know it is God's good pleasure—God's delight, God's joy—to give us the kingdom of God, we can trust our joy without dosing it in small measures. Because God made us for joy, we can laugh at the devil. Because in the midst of violence and death and upheaval and betrayal, God is still in the vineyard, and God will ensure the harvest is plentiful.

. . . .

She Who Speaks Life:*
 You are the author of our joy and the threader of
  our connection,
 because all of us, all of us, are Your children.
 Shield our joy,
 nourish our interdependence on each other,
 and give us courage to trust the goodness of our
  divine inheritance
 in You.
 Alleluia.

---

* A title for God from Rev. Wilda C. Gafney's translation of Psalm 78. (Wilda C. Gafney, "Advent II," in *A Women's Lectionary for the Whole Church: Year W* [New York: Church Publishing, 2021], Kindle.)

15

Hannah Wanted a Baby but Found Her Voice

· · · · · · · · · · · · · · · ·

My heart rejoices in the LORD.
My strength rises up in the LORD! . . .
The ones who were starving are now fat from
food!

1 SAMUEL 2:1, 5 (CEB)

The Bible is full of stories of fertility struggles. And I do not think these stories have been passed down to keep women barefoot in the kitchen—because if that were the case, Hannah would never have sassed off to a priest and then been lauded as faithful.

But I'm getting ahead of myself.

Our story begins with a family road trip for the holidays. Year after year, Hannah, her husband Elkanah, his other wife Peninnah, and Peninnah's many children go to the temple at Shiloh to make sacrifices. Going to the temple as a family was a time carved out to be particularly close to God, and it was marked by a special meal. Much like a trip to the in-laws' for Christmas, it provided time off from work to be together, with family, without distraction. Uninterrupted familial bliss, under the auspices of holiness.

But family holidays have always been a challenge, even back

then. You see, Peninnah has children. Hannah does not, even though she and Elkanah have been trying for years. And every year, in this time of togetherness, Peninnah mocks Hannah for her lack of children. This mockery is about more than the pain of an empty womb; it is a derision of Hannah's value as a person. Though her husband loves her and (unlike Peninnah) treats her with extra kindness, Hannah has not fulfilled her most essential task as a woman: to bear a child.

The moment I feel tempted to dismiss this story as irrelevant because society works differently now, I feel America Ferrera's monologue in the *Barbie* movie descend like the voice of God. Yes, women have more obvious power in modern Western culture than they did in the ancient Near East, but it's still true that we live with sickening double standards. Be a mother, but don't *long* to be a mother more than you want a career. Have children, but don't let them inconvenience your social life, sex life, work life, or looks. Love your children so self-sacrificially you lose your sense of self, but do not allow their needs to supersede your work or your marriage. And if your mental health suffers because of any of this, you just need more self-care! (Like communal care isn't even an option? We have to do *all* of this by ourselves?) So, sure, I don't live in a world that *demands* I have a son, but we're still a far cry from a world wherein women are *not* defined by having or not having children. Hannah's struggles are still relevant to us today.

By the same token, Hannah's grief over her infertility is not simply the product of living in a society without feminism. I have lived through a miscarriage. I felt embarrassed about my sadness, because we already had a child. When I told the nurse we weren't trying, she exclaimed, "Well, phew! You dodged a bullet!" That is not how it felt for me. It's certainly not how Hannah seemed to feel. Hannah is grieving. Her grief has grown, year after year after year. How many months has she hoped, only to bleed? Only to feel so empty she cannot stomach it anymore? Hannah's grief is ravenous. It gnaws away her appetite. The Bible says she "wept and would not eat" (1 Samuel 1:7).

And during this pilgrimage to the temple, Hannah snaps. She has sat through the meal, sat through Peninnah's taunts, but as everyone else clears the dishes and gets into bed, Hannah alone arises. She arises to go to the temple, the house of God, to make her plea.

When she arrives, she begins to pray, silently. The Common English Bible translation says, "Hannah was praying in her heart; her lips were moving, but her voice was silent" (1 Samuel 1:13). Hannah has lost social status by bearing no children. She has lost her appetite and her ability to rage and lament. Now, she has lost her voice. All that is left are the sighs in her heart, sighs too deep for words.

I wonder if you have ever prayed like Hannah, with sighs too deep for words. I wonder if you have ever felt so worthless that even whispering it out loud felt like it would confirm your deepest fears. I wonder if you have been like Hannah: pouring your heart out to God in a place beyond sound.

But while Hannah is praying a prayer beyond words, we are told the priest Eli is watching from "beside the doorpost of the temple of the LORD" (1 Samuel 1:9). Pay attention: Eli is watching from the *doorway*—the threshold, the passageway between the world and God's dwelling. He stands as arbitrator of who gets to come in or be cast out. And because Eli sees that Hannah's lips are moving but no sound is coming out, Eli determines that she is drunk.

So, interrupting a woman's agonized prayers, this priest says, "How long will you act like a drunk? Sober up!" (1 Samuel 1:14, CEB).

And Hannah may have lost her sense of worth, she may have lost her appetite, she may even have lost her voice, but she does *not* let this priest Eli take her prayers away from her.

Hannah answers, "No, my lord, I am a woman deeply troubled; I have drunk neither wine nor strong drink, but I have been pouring out my soul before the LORD. Do not regard your servant as a worthless woman, for I have been speaking out of my great anxiety and vexation all this time" (1 Samuel 1:15–16).

Hannah comes to the temple to plead with God for a son, and what she finds instead is her voice. Hannah's audacious, sassy reply to this priest and his (literal and figurative) gatekeeping is a moment of profound faithfulness. She knows that the pain she has offered to God is a worthy offering, even if she is a "worthless" woman.

Somewhere in the deep, unvoiced ache, I think she discovered that she deserves to be on holy ground. Maybe it was hitting rock bottom and being told she was making a spectacle of herself. Maybe it was the lie Eli accused her of—being drunk—when she was stone-cold sober and sad. Maybe it was just that Eli wasn't her family and she could let loose with him in a way she never quite could with her kin.

I imagine Eli throwing his hands up in the air, backpedaling as he replies to Hannah: "Go in peace; the God of Israel grant the petition you have made to him" (1 Samuel 1:17). Eli pleads that God grant Hannah what she was bold enough and broken enough to ask for.

And so Hannah goes home. She eats. She is no longer sad. She who had lost her appetite and her voice and her sense of self-worth finds her joy again.

She is not pregnant when she first goes home and eats and drinks. The text is very clear that it is only *after* the family has returned from their trip to the temple that Hannah conceives. So, as joyful as we know Hannah is when she gives birth to that long-awaited son, we sell her story short if we think her "happy ending" is a child. Her happy ending is baring her heart to God and knowing God hears her.

God is uniquely present with each of us in our reproductive stories, but I do not think God's sole plan for all women is mother-hood. Rather, I think God is in the business of lowliness. I think God meets us when we are most cast down and depressed and weary, and God tenderly reminds us that our belovedness cannot be outsourced. Even the deepest aches of our hearts—the things we bury, silence, fear to name—are not what determine our worthiness of standing on holy ground. These things do not make us unholy or unwanted.

And God will remind us of this—but it's on us to receive those reminders. It is on us to remember whose we are. Which means, sometimes, like Hannah, we might just have to be audacious enough, and sassy enough, and risky enough to speak up and speak out of those silenced shames. To say, *I, too, am worthy enough to stand in prayer in the house of the Most High God.*

. . . .

God who sees and is not ashamed:
You know all of who we are and all that
we can be—
and this is, frankly, terrifying.

We can be so scared to speak aloud to You what
    we know You already know. But You ask
    us to.
So here it is: we are afraid, we are angry, we are
    envious, we are sad, we are numb, we are
    greedy, we are—
we are a million things that make us feel too
    small and too big, all at once.
Remind us that You already know.
You have always known. And somehow,
You are still here.
Still.
Here, give us what we need;
give us what we don't know to ask for,
give us courage.

Help us trust where we are
    and help us see where we are going.

In the name of the groaning Spirit, the weeping
    Messiah, and the all-knowing Father,
    Amen.

· 16 ·

Born in Dazzling Darkness

· · · · · · · · · · · · · · · ·

My soul magnifies the Lord,
    and my spirit rejoices in God my Savior,
for he has looked with favor on the lowly state of
    his servant.
Surely from now on all generations will call me
    blessed,
for the Mighty One has done great things for me,
    and holy is his name.

LUKE 1:46–49

I used to be so disheartened by the Virgin Mary's, well, virginity. And: Jesus being born of the Virgin Mary is one of the core tenets of Christian belief. Her image is often the only feminine depiction of holiness in any sanctuary. And she is the most unachievable thing for a woman to be: a virgin *and* a mother.

We first meet Mary, if you follow the Orthodox tradition, as she is drawing water from a well.* An angel appears and says, "'Rejoice, favored one! The Lord is with you!' She was confused by these words and wondered what kind of greeting this might be.

---

* This detail isn't in scripture, but the chapel in Nazareth dedicated to Mary sits over a very old well, and it's a sweet connection to all the other women at wells in the Bible.

The angel said, 'Don't be afraid, Mary. God is honoring you. Look! You will conceive and give birth to a son, and you will name him Jesus'" (Luke 1:28–31, CEB). Mary asks *how*, precisely, this will come to be, as she is not married and has not had sex with her fiancé. The angel responds that the Holy Spirit "will overshadow you"—curious phrase, that—and that her cousin Elizabeth is also pregnant, "even in her old age," for "nothing is impossible for God" (Luke 1:35–37, CEB). There is so much more to this story—Mary immediately dashing off to see this cousin, and the song she sings to her cousin about God, which we call the Magnificat.

But what you hear the most about is her virginity.

Partially, this is patriarchy at work. The concept that the penetrative actions of a man can irrevocably change and lessen a woman—which is how "losing your virginity" is often presented to us—reduces sex to something one-dimensional, when the reality is that sex is something we can unfurl into, little by little, trusting and exploring and receiving and giving. To paraphrase Rowan Williams, the former Archbishop of Canterbury, sex, at its holiest, is being open and changed by the profound grace of wanting and being wanted as we are, naked, body and soul.

Mother Mary has always been taught to me as especially sacred because she was so "pure." The angel never calls her pure, though; the angel says nothing is impossible for God. The emphasis is on the Holy Spirit *overshadowing* Mary—again, curious language!—and filling her with this promise and impossibility. Her virginity is ancillary to God doing the impossible.

And yet: virgin birth. It matters. One Advent, during my college church internship, I was midway through leading a Bible study on Mary, popping off about the evils of patriarchal definitions of hymens, when a friend of mine quietly said, "Look, I agree that her virginity is overblown. But I think it matters that she did not know what she was doing and had the courage to say yes anyway." This stopped me in my tracks in that moment. It does still.

Because as much as I want to control all that happens to me, the reality remains: faith means we don't know the ending. We can never, ever fully *know* what we're getting into. Love takes risk—motherhood perhaps most of all. What if the person I am making this baby with leaves me? What if our love falls apart? What if I can't get pregnant? What if my baby is sick? What if I lose this pregnancy? And what happens once the baby arrives—how will I live through my child's losses, pains? What if I have a baby I adore and a marriage that is beautiful and our baby dies? What then?

Love takes risk. Motherhood takes risk. And God knows this most of all, because God made us, knowing all that would and could unfold, and did it anyway. So perhaps Jesus being born of the Virgin Mary is less about women and sex and more about God being willing to try something new for the sake of new creation.

After all, Creation began in the dark, with the Spirit hovering over the deep in Genesis 1. New Creation begins in the dark, too—this time, the darkness of Mary's womb, and the darkness of her knowing-and-unknowing.

God is no stranger to doing dazzling things in the darkness. Theologian Sarah Coakley makes the case that one of the most ancient ways we come to know God is through the disorientation of darkness. Drawing on the work of Cappadocian mystic and bishop Saint Gregory of Nyssa, she says that "human spiritual advance towards intimacy with God as Trinity ultimately leads to an unnerving 'darkness'—the 'darkness of incomprehensibility.'"

She comes to call this darkness "dazzling," because to walk into the intimacy of God's darkness is to be dazzled and disoriented from what we know, from our certainties, and from being silenced into the power of contemplative unknowing and wonder.

And no person was more intimate with God than Mary. Mary consents to the dazzling darkness of God to be about her, but also within her very womb.

Advent, the church season when we anticipate Christmas with Mary, is a season when, as Cole Arthur Riley writes, "we make space for darkness" and "think about a God who dwelled in the sacred Blackness of a womb before being born into the world at Christmas." While darkness is so often maligned and equated to evil—with disastrous sociological and psychological results—it can actually be a place of sacred encounter. Indeed, in the Incarnation of Jesus Christ, God sees fit not only to dwell in a body but to come into the world through the body and blood of a woman. (As Sojourner Truth said, "And how came Jesus into the world? Through God who created him and woman who bore him. Man, where is your part?")

Mary is bold enough to say, "Let it be with me according to your word," as she receives the Word into her womb (Luke 1:38). Perhaps her virginity is not rooted in being unblemished but in embracing the dazzling darkness of not knowing—and choosing to be hopeful, anyway.

And maybe it is because *we* know the ending of the story that we so want to make meaning of Mary knowing or not knowing. We know Mary's story will include tremendous pain when she watches her son die on the cross. Did you know, Mary? All that you were signing up to endure? Of course, Mary did know some things. She knew that God had lifted up the lowly and filled the hungry with good things. She knew who her son, the Son, was. But she still could not know all the contours of what was to come.

It is a question I think parenthood asks of all of us: Did you know that all this joy would also mean all this pain? It is an *unhinged* risk to bring a baby into your life, whether by birth, adoption, fostering, or caring for a child in your extended family or community. Allowing yourself to love this fragile creature is terrifying. The only thing you know for sure is that they'll die— hopefully in a far-off someday, but maybe far too soon. And we give birth, we love, we welcome children anyway. We make life knowing life ends. That is wild.

And parenthood is not the only relationship that demands this kind of risk, nor is motherhood the only story for which Mary's courage can be a banner for us. All love takes risk. Choosing any new and uncharted path takes risk. Anytime we face a situation in which, though we might have an inkling of what lies ahead, we do not know (or really, cannot know) what will unfold, Mary is the beacon who can enflame our courage for the unknown and the daunting.

Mary said yes to God, knowing who God is, but not knowing what God would do. And Mary's joy is not doomed by the sorrow that will also come.

So how can Mary's unknowing but wholehearted courage lead us? How can we, like Mary, trust in the darkness of a womb and in the dazzling darkness of a woman saying yes anyway? Because the yes Mary offers is a yes that opens the revolution of the world. And the Magnificat she sings about her yes to God is a song about her motherhood, but it is also ultimately about the new world God is making through her in each of us when we take the risk of saying yes to God's wild ideas.

. . . .

Our souls magnify our God,
   and our spirits rejoice in the dazzling darkness
      wherein You move.
   Surely, all is not for us to understand,
   but all is held in the palm of Your hand.

Like You there is no one,
   wanting a world where there was none,
   incarnating creation
   within a warrior-woman's fragile body.

Help us believe You when You say:
   Behold: I am doing something new.
   Bridle our teeth with courage to say:
   Us, too?

In the name of the God
   who brings down the powerful,
   lifts up the lowly,
   and remembers Her promises forever:
   Amen.

PART III

Liberating Jesus

MYTH: To be saved, Christians have always been required to have a personal relationship with Jesus that begins when one can consciously pray for Jesus to come into one's heart.

MYSTERY: A personal relationship with Jesus is something we are born being offered, whether we ever have the conscious mind to know it or not. Jesus asks us to know him in the breaking of bread and loving of neighbors and in worshipping our Sovereign God.

I don't remember exactly where I was the first time it happened, but I do remember the discomfort at the lingering eye contact and the accompanying pamphlet. I was being asked: *Have you accepted Jesus into your heart?* It was a weird question to ask a ten-year-old. It's a weird question to ask a grown woman in a clergy collar doing her grocery run after work, too, but somehow I still can't go more than a month or so without *someone* asking me if I've accepted Jesus into my heart.

As a ten-year-old, I remember

being wildly confused. Accepted Jesus? I had never known this was a choice—not in the sense that I felt I had no autonomy but in the sense that I had never, not once, felt like I lived *apart* from God. God was everywhere and everything to me. We talked when I ambled through the woods with the latest *Harry Potter* tucked under my arm, heading to my spot in the tree that slung over the creek to read all afternoon. We looked for angels together on every cross-country flight I took (I hadn't yet given up hope that I might at least see one wing peeping out behind a cloud). I used to lie to my mother about choir practice—I told her it started a whole ten minutes before its actual start time—just so that I could sneak into the sanctuary and lie prostrate on the ground in front of the giant crucifix at the altar.

I mean, I was a weird kid. And I was a weird kid because of Jesus and my obsession with him. I don't know "when" I made the "choice" to "accept Jesus into my heart" as a child, and such logic is predicated on cognitive ability in a way that makes me sad. I've been a hospice chaplain; I have kept vigil over people whose cognitive capacity to choose most things was long gone. I've held many newborn babies whose only instincts seemed to be for milk and Mama and snuggling. All of these people knew God, even if they hadn't "chosen" or could not remember "choosing" God in this one very particular way.

To choose to follow Jesus is a beautiful choice, but if that is the whole point of following Jesus, we have reduced our Savior to our own cognitive capacities. Jesus promised us a relationship, but he also promised us mysteries: to show up in such mysterious things as "the breaking of bread" and in prison and as naked, needy people.

In this section, we'll focus on liberating Jesus Christ from the myths we often tell about him as we dive into the unfathomably beautiful mystery of who Jesus really is.

Mother of God, Dethroner of Dragons

....

And Elizabeth was filled with the Holy Spirit and exclaimed with a loud cry, "Blessed are you among women, and blessed is the fruit of your womb. And why has this happened to me, that the mother of my Lord comes to me? For as soon as I heard the sound of your greeting, the child in my womb leaped for joy. And blessed is she who believed that there would be a fulfillment of what was spoken to her by the Lord."

LUKE 1:41–45

In the fall of 2023, my husband, our then-eighteen-month-old daughter, and I spent three days at a big, mandatory, multiday meeting with all of my regional Episcopal clergy colleagues. My daughter interrupted every keynote presentation with squawks of "No, Mama!" She wiggled free from her stroller, our laps, our small enclave of chairs and friends fencing her in to tot-trot toward each speaker. All three of us changed outfits three times a day, every day, to get rid of the reek of toddler-smeared sweet potato.

We are really, really blessed with incredible colleagues and bishops who helped carry the diaper bag or took a turn rolling around on the floor with her during a talk, or even interrupted their annual address to say that she was no bother. They said they were glad she was there, and we believe them. Still, by the end of three days of trying to be priest and a mom and a person without our regular routine to sustain us, I was depleted.

As I was wrapping up breakfast with my friend Madre Minerva, she began stacking my family's many oozing dishes onto her tray, waving away my attempt to help clean up our enormous toddler breakfast mess. "I remember these days!" she exclaimed knowingly, smiling.

I exhaled in relief. "What would we do without other moms?"

She paused, looked me in the eye, and said, "Lizzie, without other moms, there would be no more moms."

If that is not the truth, I don't know what is.

And honestly, it explains to me why, in Luke 1, the first thing Mary does after she has spoken with the angel Gabriel about this business of carrying the Messiah into the world is to march her first-trimester body one hundred miles away to the Judean hill country to see her cousin Elizabeth.

In the story of the Annunciation, an oft overlooked detail is that the angel Gabriel says: *Nothing will be impossible for God, because—get this! Your cousin Elizabeth? The old one? She, too, is having a miraculous experience of pregnancy, parallel to yours.* Elizabeth is past the age of having children, yet God has given her and her husband Zechariah a child, even though she was said to be barren. God assures Mary in this moment of total newness that there is still some companionship, some precedent. Because God understands that mamas need other mamas.

So as Mary enters the first weeks of her divine pregnancy, Elizabeth is entering her third trimester of a not-quite-as-miraculous-but-still-holy pregnancy. And as soon as the angel departs from Mary, she makes the hundred-mile journey (presumably on foot) to her cousin Elizabeth. And while walking a hundred miles seems awful in the absolute hellscape that is the first trimester of pregnancy, I also totally get why Mary does this. What she's going through is so wild, so terrifying, and so beautiful that she will go to any lengths to be with someone who is going through the same thing.

And when Mary appears on Elizabeth's doorstep, surely coated with dust from a trying journey, Elizabeth's child leaps in her womb at the sound of Mary's voice. Elizabeth comes running—or waddling—to greet her and hails Mary with the words "Blessed are you among women, and blessed is the fruit of your womb" (Luke 1:42).

If you, like me, grew up Roman Catholic, these words might sound familiar, as they're the basis of the Hail Mary prayer. But there is more to this line than we often acknowledge: Elizabeth knows her Bible. Elizabeth is putting Mary in a long line of heroines by greeting her with words traditionally used to describe women who have, by the power of God, literally slain their enemies.

In the book of Judges, an Israelite woman named Yael kills an enemy general called Sisera by plying him with milk, covering him with a blanket, and then, right as he falls asleep, driving a tent peg through his head. This allows the Israelite army to triumph over the Canaanite army, prompting the prophetess Deborah to sing a song describing Yael as "most blessed of women" (Judges 5:24).

In the book of Judith,* Judith similarly plies the enemy general Holofernes with alcohol, and when he passes out, she decapitates him. As Judith holds up his severed head so her city can see they've been saved from invasion, King Uzziah says: "O daughter, you are blessed by the Most High God above all other women on earth" (Judith 13:18).

Elizabeth is placing Mary in this lineage of women who have beheaded and stabbed powerful military men—and Mary has not beheaded anyone but has instead conceived a child. Elizabeth sees an almost military heroism in her cousin Mary. Because an old, married pregnant woman is calling a young, unmarried pregnant woman a *warrior* before the dust from her journey has even settled, as the two of them are alone and breathless from their expanding wombs and from all that the breath of God has done in them.

This is a revelation. A revolution.

I am far from the first to see Elizabeth calling Mary a slayer of enemies, a warrior in the lineage of Yael and Judith. Religious scholar Lauren Winner writes that some "readings of the beginning of Luke suggest that Mary does indeed kill . . . what she kills is her own will. And a long history of visual interpretation shows Mary killing the serpent. In many renderings of Our Lady of Guadalupe, the pregnant Mary is stepping on the serpent, killing it—specifically crushing its head, as Yael crushed Sisera's head with a tent peg." Indeed, in many artistic renderings, the serpent looks more like a dragon or a fearsome sea creature. In some of my favorite illuminated manuscripts from the Middle Ages, Mary is seen wrestling the dragonish devil to the ground (sometimes while

---

* The book of Judith is deuterocanonical, and is included in Catholic and Orthodox Bibles.

an obliging angel stands nearby, holding an infant Jesus who cheers on his mighty mama).

Mary may be the one we (rightly) revere, the one who brings God into the world as her own child, by the power of the God who made her. But all warriors need other warriors to endure.

All moms need other moms. I suspect Mary needed Elizabeth.

Elizabeth's revolution is quiet, often overshadowed by the impressive son she bears (John the Baptist) and her celebrity cousin. But her witness is in her very name, because the name Elizabeth means "the promise of God." Elizabeth, with Mary, prefigures and echoes the women who will be the first witnesses and preachers of the Resurrection—for they are the first witnesses and preachers of the Incarnation.

Not one woman. *Women.*

And Elizabeth says to Mary—and to all of us, the quiet rebels and the wielders of tent pegs alike—"Blessed is she who believed that there would be a fulfillment of what was spoken to her by the Lord" (Luke 1:45).

. . . .

Blessed God,
> who entered this world by the blood and water
> > of a woman,
> and whose side poured forth blood and water
> as she watched You die on the cross,
> bless us to believe nothing is impossible with
> > and for You.
> In the wars of our hearts and in the wars of our
> > world
> tear down the mighty from their thrones,

lift up the lowly,
and fill our hunger with Your goodness.
For You are our liberator,
our emancipator,
and our invigorator,
Amen.

· 18 ·

Joseph and the Courage to Not Be the Main Character

. . . .

> As he was thinking about this, an angel from the
> Lord appeared to him in a dream and said, "Joseph
> son of David, don't be afraid to take Mary as your
> wife, because the child she carries was conceived
> by the Holy Spirit."
>
> MATTHEW 1:20 (CEB)

When I was in the fifth grade, my parents left our Catholic church and started worshipping at a new church, a Methodist one with big stained glass windows and a preacher who remembered our names. Which was fine for them, but we started at this new church during Advent, which meant *someone else had already been cast as Mary in the Christmas pageant.*

I was gutted. But, ever the pragmatist, I thought of the next largest part in the play: Jesus! But . . . he's a baby and doesn't say much. Not ideal. Next on the list was Joseph. I politely asked my Sunday school teacher if I could play Joseph, please, if he hadn't been cast already. Unbeknownst to me, this caused a stir in the children's ministry. A little girl wanting to be Joseph? Two girls

playing the Holy Family couple?? Apparently this was so trans-
gressive that pastors were called—which I know because, over a
decade later, my best friend worked for this very church and people were *still talking about it.*

Listen, I'd love to claim it was a brave rebellion against gender
norms (and it was, a bit), but really, I just wanted a starring role.
But the funny thing is, though Joseph—played that year by a re-
luctant *boy* whom I bitterly watched mumble his lines from my
corner of the stage as Shepherd #6—occupies an enormous part in
our telling of the Christmas story, he never actually says a word in
the Bible.

We hear from Jesus's mother, Mary, many times in the Bible,
and not just in her interactions with the angel and Elizabeth.
Throughout Jesus's life, Mary speaks. When the boy Jesus runs
away from his parents in Jerusalem, it is Mary who says, "Child,
why have you treated us like this? Listen! Your father and I have
been worried. We've been looking for you!" (Luke 2:48, CEB). In
the Gospel of John, it is Mary who gently admonishes Jesus into
his first public miracle: turning water into wine. She is with him
through his crucifixion, and she is there at the empty tomb when
he is raised from the dead; she is there for Pentecost and the birth
of the church.

It is safe to say that Mary, for all the ways she is a serene and
resplendent reflection of God's gentleness and love, is no shrinking
violet. She is an outspoken, brave, flawed, beautiful mother whom
we do actually hear quite a bit from—which is remarkable, given
how often the women in the Bible are either silent or subsumed
under their husbands' or fathers' words and willpower. So it is interesting to me that Joseph—Mary's husband, Jesus's earthly
father—never directly utters a word in the entirety of the Bible.

But that doesn't mean he fades into the background of the story or that we don't know anything about him. We are told Joseph is a "righteous man" who is unwilling to humiliate his betrothed when he finds out she's pregnant (Matthew 1:19, CEB). Being the respectable small business owner and pillar of the community that he is, "he wanted to divorce her secretly" (Matthew 1:19). He wants to protect Mary as much as possible from public scandal—but he also wants to distance himself from the perceived impropriety in her pregnancy before marriage. (The challenge of figuring out how to achieve that in a small town like Nazareth might be why he takes some time to deliberate.) And while Mary gets an angelic visit calling her blessed and favored, Joseph gets an angelic call telling him, basically, to stop being afraid and get his booty back in line: "As he was thinking about this, an angel from the Lord appeared to him in a dream and said, 'Joseph son of David, don't be afraid to take Mary as your wife, because the child she carries was conceived by the Holy Spirit'" (Matthew 1:20, CEB).

God intervenes and reveals to Joseph a truth that is wild, and unpredictable, and disorderly, a truth that means Joseph is not only being charged with marrying Mary but also with raising a child he knows is not his biological kin.* The miracle of the Christmas story is Jesus, of course, but I think the big miracle of Joseph's story is that *he changes his mind*. He allows God's truth to transform him. He realizes his assumptions about Mary were wrong, and he makes a courageous, costly, clear decision to cast his lot with her.

---

* You may have heard it said blood is thicker than water, but as my husband (and fellow priest) Jonathan says, the waters of baptism are thicker than blood. I think Joseph's love for Jesus prefigures what we all experience in baptism, because Joseph's love is thicker than blood. Joseph is also often seen as the patron saint of foster and adoptive parents.

Joseph, like his Old Testament namesake, heeds his dreams from God. He is a good man who relinquishes his safety, his privilege, even his voice for the greater story of what God is doing in and through the margins. Just because he isn't as central to the story as Mary doesn't mean he's not central to God's love; rather, his journey teaches us that when we are called to lay down what is comfortable for the sake of God's revolution, God sees and God cares. Joseph is not ancillary to the story; instead, he shows us what can happen in our lives when we let God be the main character.

And Joseph's story asks: What could happen if we, like Joseph, choose not to quietly disassociate from scandal, choose not to wash our hands of a situation and walk away, but instead embrace the scandal and mess and beauty of God choosing us? What might happen if we allow the truth to change our minds, to alter our course, to radically reshape what we thought was just? What might happen if we allow God to be the main character in our lives and in the lives of everyone around us?

. . . .

God, our Father:
    You have steadfastly loved us,
    over and over,
    even when we were afraid to let Your love
        transform us.

Help us be like Your servant, Joseph:
    quietly present,
    loudly trusting,

willing to risk our relative safety for the sake of
the Good News.

Help us have the courage to change our minds
and to change course,
when we are torn between what we were told
was right
and the justice our dreams have longed for.

Remind us that even when we are not
acknowledged
for our risk and sacrifice,
You, our Father, have seen us in secret and will
reward us.

Thank You for being Good News
for all of us.

Amen.

19

Backwoods Empire

. . . .

> Nearby shepherds were living in the fields, guard-
> ing their sheep at night. The Lord's angel stood be-
> fore them, the Lord's glory shone around them, and
> they were terrified. The angel said, "Don't be
> afraid! Look! I bring good news to you—wonderful,
> joyous news for all people. Your savior is born to-
> day in David's city. He is Christ the Lord. This is a
> sign for you: you will find a newborn baby wrapped
> snugly and lying in a manger."
>
> LUKE 2:8–12 (CEB)

The Christmas story is so well-worn it is easy to miss how unhinged it actually is. Away in a manger, no crib for a bed? Sure, we
know this story. Cattle lowing, angels glowing, shepherds in the
fields where it was snowing. An idyllic nativity, a birth so predictable we put tinsel on it every year.

Except nothing about Christmas was well-worn or predictable.

We sing the songs and don our sweaters and wrangle children
into sheep costumes, and we *think* we know this story. But what
happens if we look at the Christmas story in its raw edges, without the glimmering lights and cocoa?

In the Magnificat, Jesus's mother, Mary, sang about God tearing the mighty off their thrones and lifting up the lowly. Was she imagining that Jesus would lead an actual army reclaiming their people's stolen land from the clutches of the Roman Empire? Certainly, many thought that was the purpose of the Messiah. Many still do—imagine Christ as conqueror, that is. And yet, even before this Messiah was born, this same empire displaced his parents; even when Mary was enormous with child, she and Joseph were forced to go to Bethlehem. The ruler in charge was Caesar Augustus, and he demanded that they be counted in a census for taxes. I guess the two guarantees in life were true, even for Jesus: death and taxes.

But another kind of reign was coming, because another kind of king was born—not in hallowed halls, or even in a home of his own. Emmanuel, our Sovereign, was born on the floor where the animals were kept because there was no room elsewhere.

We, hearing this story, are spared the gory details of labor. It's like the camera pans to the scene of shepherds in a field, where angels interrupt a quiet evening to terrify the shepherds by blaring good news. Though in every nativity set I see, the shepherds are all grown men, anthropologically and biblically speaking, we can assume many were also women and girls.* Shepherds were not distinguished guests ornamenting the halls of power where emperors were born. They were more like the night-shift workers at a big-box store, restocking shelves in the wee hours. And still: *Go!* the angels demand. *Go and see this baby! Good news!* God is turning all the predictable means of power inside out, upside down. Smelly

---

* Rachel was a shepherd (Genesis 29:9), and Zipporah and her sisters were shepherds (Exodus 2:16).

shepherds, fresh from the hard ground, kneeling before a feeding trough become the epicenter of a revolution.

And in that feeding trough there is a king born as a vulnerable child, wrapped in swaddling clothes and lying in a manger. A king, dressed in linens that foreshadow: someday, his fragile body will be wrapped in cloths and laid in a tomb. A Messiah, sleeping in a feeding trough that foreshadows: someday, he will offer his body as food for all his children. God, womb of life, crafter of the universe—held in this Christ child, a squalling infant with a full diaper.

Pull aside the tinsel and lights to really pay attention to this child, born under the rubble of empire, and see: Christmas is actually, rudely unpredictable. No one saw this story coming. From the beginning Jesus makes it known that God is doing a *new* thing.

Christmas is not the story we know, even as it very much is, because Christmas is a tender revolution. It is tempting to let the holiday lights and shopping lists inoculate us against the power of Christmas. It is understandable that hearing this story over and over would make us think the baby Jesus in the manger in Bethlehem is inevitable. But it is not.

Christmas upends what kingship looks like, where power resides, and who matters. Christmas is a subversion in which the backwoods nowhere of an empire is made holy. Christmas is a story in which the only person who knows what comes next is God, and the rest of us are invited into deeper trust and surrender as we follow *a baby* for salvation.

What would our relationship to power look like if we imagined real power in the form of that infant Christ in a cradle? What might we reexamine about our existence if we knew God shows

up in the backwoods of our own lives, ready to feed us with unexpected nourishment?

....

Sovereign God:
　　Your law is love, and Your Gospel is peace—
　　teach us to hear old things made new.
　　Rattle our assumption-cages,
　　open our eyes to the work You have been doing
　　　　all along
　　in the places and people we didn't think
　　were important enough for our noticing.
　　Thank You for trusting us
　　with Your infant body,
　　for showing us that Your faith in us
　　gives us the greatest gift
　　of faith in You.
　　We know Your revolution will upend the world
　　into something even more beautiful than we
　　　　can imagine.
　　Let us be a part of it,
　　in the name of Christ, tender and mild
　　　　revolutionary.
　　Amen.

20

Jesus Loves
a Sloppy Disco

. . . .

On the third day there was a wedding in Cana of
Galilee. Jesus' mother was there, and Jesus and his
disciples were also invited to the celebration. When
the wine ran out, Jesus' mother said to him, "They
don't have any wine."

JOHN 2:1–3 (CEB)

If ever you doubt that Jesus Christ was "truly God and truly human," look no further than the way he gripes at his mother in John
chapter 2. John 1:14 (CEB) says, "The Word became flesh and made
his home among us," underscoring the fact that Jesus did not live
with us just to bide his time before revealing his human skin
as a costume. No: God, true God from true God, "made his home
among us" as a human. And like all humans, he had a fight with
his mom at a family party.

John chapter 2 begins like this: "On the third day there was a
wedding in Cana of Galilee. Jesus' mother was there, and Jesus
and his disciples were also invited to the celebration" (John 2:1–2,
CEB). For those of us who grew up in the church or are just famil-

iar with the most famous Bible stories, it is easy to skip right over those first four words—we know, after all, that there is a miracle impending: Jesus is going to turn water into wine. But the Gospel of John never misses an opportunity to link the mundane with the enchantment of God. And so the first four words—*On the third day*—are a clue that what is about to happen at this wedding is linked to what is *ultimately* going to happen: God is going to harrow hell. Defeat death. Walk out of a stale tomb, scarred but alive.

But before he does all that, he's at a big family wedding in Cana, and, halfway through the party, the hosts run out of wine. A devastating faux pas. The disco ball has just been lowered and the DJ just broke out the Motown! We need wine, and we all know that the corner store is closed right now!

And Mary, Mother of God, goes to her son and says, "They don't have any wine" (John 2:3, CEB). And Jesus retorts, "What does that have to do with me? My time hasn't come yet" (John 2:4, CEB). The Son is sassing back to his mother. Truly: human.

Maybe Mary wants Jesus to do this because she knows he can; maybe, as a toddler, he transformed his lentils into olives (what *was* it like raising God?!). Or maybe she, like all moms, knows sometimes our children need just a little nudge to launch into all we know they can be. I imagine Mary plucking a piece of lint from Jesus's tunic before she saunters back to the fretting mother of the bride, airily telling the servants, "Do whatever he tells you" (John 2:5, CEB).

So whether he does it while rolling his eyes and complaining to his Father about his mom, or whether he does it with complete command and calm, Jesus turns the water into wine.

This is an *enormous* amount of water—six stone jars that each hold "about twenty or thirty gallons" (John 2:6, CEB). And when it becomes wine, it is not just bottom-shelf Franzia. It's the good stuff, the kind of wine my husband and I buy once or twice a year for special date nights—the head waiter actually compliments the groom for busting out the better wine later in the party.

John 2:6 notes that the stone jars Jesus uses are intended to be "used for the Jewish cleansing ritual" (CEB), meaning this water was originally meant to purify the household according to the Law. But the fact that Jesus has turned it into wine does not mean he's saying people don't need to be purified. Remember, purification is about God knowing, and caring, that our bodies change.

What Jesus shows us with this miracle is that God gave us bodies so we can *live* in them. And God can show up when we're shaking down. Sometimes we become our purest selves when we embrace our joy at the deepest, wildest level. Jesus's truest humanity beckons our truest humanity. Because Jesus Christ loves a sloppy party. The kind of party where the good wine comes out right at the hinge moment, when people decide if they're going to dip early or kick off their shoes and boogie down on the dance floor.

Obviously, alcohol is not always good for us, and the point of this story is not that we should all get blitzed in the name of Jesus. But I think Jesus is saying here what God has said over and over in the Bible: to honor God who gives us life and life abundant is to live our lives fully, loving our bodies by dancing with fervor and eating rich foods and drinking sweet wine.* God wants to ensure

---

* See also Nehemiah 8:10, Leviticus 25, John 10:10, Isaiah 55:1–3, John 15:11, Psalm 23:1, Ecclesiastes 9:7, Psalm 136:25, etc.

that no one goes hungry. That includes the poor who cannot af-
ford to eat as well as the anxiously self-denied. God probes into
our self-loathing and says, *Babe, have the treat.* Everyone is fed in
the kingdom of God. Everyone gets to drink the good wine in the
kingdom of God.

In his first act of public ministry, Jesus is showing us the end is
resurrection. Because, my God, is resurrection not found on the
dance floor? In the late-night buzz of a wedding? Is our God not
the God who is resurrected early in the morning that third day
when the hours are blurred from after-midnight into predawn?
Yes. Yes, our God is.

Resurrection is prefigured in singing along to Whitney Houston
at the top of your lungs alongside your grandma and your little
second cousin who is up way past their bedtime. Resurrection happens in the afterparty at the gay bar as the two brides lead us in a
conga line. Resurrection happens when two brothers who have
warred with each other for years decide to loosen their ties, pull
up chairs on the fringes of the reception, and hash it out for the
sake of the family's peace.

Resurrection happens when the Word made Flesh makes a
home among us.

. . . .

God whose love
    was a fragrant sacrifice to God,*
    thank You for our bodies,
    thank You for good music,

* Ephesians 5:2.

thank You for the gift it is to taste, to smell, to
    see, to touch, to be held, and to be free.
Thank You for the gift of joy, of connection, of
    sweet release and sweeter reuniting.
Help us remember that sometimes, to meet You,
    we must unclench our hold on life and let
    You lead us on the dance floor,
help us remember Your purification of our
    bodies can come when we eat the rich
    foods and drink the sweet wines,
and give us the courage to trust that You will
    never let the party collapse.
In the name of God triune,
Dancer, Dreamer, Doer,
Amen.

21

Being Born Again
Is About Being a Baby

·················

Jesus answered him, "Very truly, I tell you, no one can see the kingdom of God without being born from above." Nicodemus said to him, "How can anyone be born after having grown old? Can one enter a second time into the mother's womb and be born?"

JOHN 3:3–4

Nicodemus comes to him under the cover of night. Far from prying eyes, prying ears. Jesus has been making a stir. And Nicodemus is a Pharisee. The word Pharisee has a negative connotation among many Christians, largely because of unexamined anti-Semitism. Pharisees were Jewish religious leaders in Jesus's day. When he argues with them, it's not because they're evil or because their theology is diametrically opposed to his—it's more like a debate in a seminary classroom.

Nicodemus recognizes the truth in Jesus's message, but like all institutional leaders, his fear of change is real. His need to take time to absorb it all is real. And his desire to retreat into the shadows to think it through is *clearly* real, because he comes to Jesus cloaked in the anonymity of night.

And Nicodemus says to Jesus, basically, *I know you are of God because no one can do what you are doing apart from God.*

And Jesus, ever infuriating, responds, "No one can enter the kingdom of God without being born of water and Spirit" (John 3:5).*

This is a patently *weird* thing to say. But in many modern Christian spaces, the weirdness is never examined. Christians have heard the phrase "born again" so often that it feels . . . predictable. Inevitable. Almost like the "gotcha" we saw coming from a mile away. But to Nicodemus, who has never seen John 3:16 written on a T-shirt, this is more than a bit of a zag.

I like to imagine Nicodemus is so thrown he almost laughs: *It's impossible to enter into a mother's womb for a second time, Jesus! No one can be "born again."* But then he catches a glimpse of Jesus's utterly serious face. With dawning horror, he says, *It's impossible to enter into a mother's womb and be born again . . . right? Jesus?*

So Jesus explains: "I assure you, unless someone is born of water and the Spirit, it's not possible to enter God's kingdom. Whatever is born of the flesh is flesh, and whatever is born of the Spirit is spirit. Don't be surprised that I said to you, 'You must be born anew'" (John 3:5–7, CEB).

Some teach this verse like Jesus is saying: *You were born of the flesh of your mother, but now you must be born of the Spirit of your Father.* But to reduce Jesus's poetic response to a mechanistic set of instructions—first be born of the flesh, then later be born of the

---

* This can also be translated as "born from above"—the word is ambiguous in the original Greek.

Spirit, which is the superior birth—neglects that Jesus was also born of flesh. The Word was made Flesh. And God made us, flesh and soul, as flesh-spirit creatures in God's image.

So what's up with these two births, then?

I've given birth. It was a spiritual bodily experience. I could not separate the presence of God in my body from the presence of God in my soul when they cut me open to pull my daughter from my womb. Birth is primal. Birth is wild. Birth is *gross*. There is blood and shit and mucus and sweat and tears and blinding pain and gorgeous release. I know—better than Nicodemus, I wager—how impossible it would be to be born again in such literal terms. And even after being literally cut open to bring my baby into this world, I sometimes feel so overwhelmed with love for my daughter I bundle her up into a little ball in my arms, blowing raspberries on her tummy, and wonder how she ever fit inside my torso. How I made her, so curious and wise and tough.

I remember what it was like to share my flesh with her—the early flutters, her tumbling in my tummy while I preached—moments I treasure but that she will never have any memory of. I remember the months I spent creating her. I remember giving birth to her. But she will not remember being born—because in birth, the baby isn't the one doing the hardest work. When we are born, *it is our mother who does the laboring*. And the way we are born of flesh ought to give us a clue as to how we are to be born spiritually.

Much like the last century-plus of medicine and parenting, the last century-plus of Christianity has focused so much on the baby (us) being born again that it has neglected to think about the Mother (Christ) giving birth. But the truth is, babies don't *do* very much in the birth process. It is the muscles and willpower and body of the *person giving birth* that push the baby out (or, in my case, a team of medical caregivers who performed a Caesarean section). The baby is not the one who is doing the labor. The baby's body can be contorted, reshaped—but the baby is simply born.

And if Jesus says we are to be born of flesh and spirit, then our task is to be a baby. And the baby's only job, really, in birth, is to trust the body of our mother as we undergo the strange and shocking revelation of being expelled from a comfortable, dark womb into the vivid daylight of the world.

In my faith tradition, the Episcopal Church, this is what we believe about baptism: it is not so much about us choosing God as it is about seeing and receiving that God has chosen *us*. And God chooses all of us. All we have to do is surrender to being chosen, to receive the love that is freely offered. But to surrender is not a passive action; it is a conscious, agency-filled choice rooted in trust of the person one is surrendering to. In our case, that is Jesus. We do not manufacture, create, or control our own births, which is why I am so grateful Jesus is the one who does the birthing-again.

I am *far* from being the first faithful Christian to see Christ as our Mother. The great mystic and saint Julian of Norwich wrote a lot about the blood and motherhood of Jesus Christ in the fourteenth century. In her book *Revelations of Divine Love*, she says, "And our Saviour is our true mother in whom we are eternally born and by whom we shall always be enclosed." Or, translated more literally from her Middle English, Christ is our true mother in whom we are eternally born, and we shall "never come out of him."

I have borne my child—my heart, my life—into this world knowing this world will hurt her. Knowing she will die. Terrified she will die before me—a newborn skull is so fragile, cars drive so fast, too many people have guns. I have borne my daughter for death. I have borne her more for life, but her inevitable death haunts me. As Julian writes, "Our mothers bear us for pain and death, but our true mother, Jesus, bears us for joy and endless life." Thinking of Jesus as our true Mother is not meant to demean the labor of mothering here on earth, but to give us comfort in the fact that we are in Christ, always. Even in death. Even when we go where our mothers cannot, even if, God forbid, our child goes where we cannot yet follow.

In Christ we are being remade, contorted and changed and challenged to grow. And, at the same time, we never ever leave the safety of the womb of God. Because none of us were born apart from God. And Jesus Christ, who is in us and around us and through us, gave birth to us because "God so loved the world that he gave his only Son, so that everyone who believes in him won't perish but will have eternal life" (John 3:16, CEB).

. . . .

Christ, our Mother,
        in whom we are endlessly born,
        and out of whom we never come—
        hold us close. Birth is terrifying.
        For the new thing, give us courage.
        For the hard thing, give us conviction.
        For the reshaping we are undergoing,
        give us a trust in the process.
        Help us let go and let You do what You do best:
        love us.
        In the name of love, birthing, being, and
                beholding—
        Amen.

22

The Tenacity of
a Bleeding Woman

....

For she said within herself, If I may but touch his
garment, I shall be whole.

MATTHEW 9:21 (KJV)

The early days of Jesus's ministry crackle with chaos. He constantly does the unexpected—like dining at the home of his new friend, Matthew, the tax collector. This alone is scandalous: Matthew is a Jew, a member of the people of Judea who have spent the last several centuries colonized and subjugated by foreign powers, most recently the Roman Empire. But Matthew is also a tax collector, which means his people regard him, fairly or not, as a traitor, because he gives their tax money to an idolatrous bully of a dictatorship, while taking a cut for himself. Essentially, tax collectors were known to have the boot of the empire on their necks, too . . . but they were willing to betray their own for a little more oxygen. And yet Jesus has called Matthew to follow him, and this sycophant has left his booth behind without a word to follow the Prince of Peace instead of the principal returns on his empire investment.

And at this dinner party at Matthew's house, all manner of

people join Jesus at the table, including the Pharisees. Pharisees are respected religious leaders who feel genuine—and frankly, righteous—indignation at Jesus's association with this traitorous tax collector. As I mentioned in the previous devotion, Pharisees are often painted with an anti-Semitic brush even by well-meaning Christians, because the scriptures show them arguing with Jesus—but in many ways, these arguments are parallel to the ones I had in seminary with my peers who were also becoming priests. (Honestly, no one fights more viciously than professional God-fearers!)

And so this dinner is unfolding with witty God-talk repartee—only to be interrupted when a respected leader in the synagogue comes crashing through the party, begging Jesus to resurrect his dead daughter. He is a father who has just endured the absolute worst thing a parent can endure: the loss of a child. He is wild-eyed and panicked. Forget being a respected leader. If this magic man they call Jesus from backwater-nowhere-Nazareth can save his little girl, he'll do anything. Anything.

Jesus gets up, and the crowd closes in behind him, his disciples following him as he walks to this man's house. They're hoping to see a miracle but preparing for a tragedy. It's a Hollywood moment: Jesus walks alongside a grieving father, surrounded by a crowd of people. Some of these people are hopeful, some are voyeurs, some are outright furious, some are skeptical, and some are curious.

And then, in the midst of this crowd of hopeful, skeptical, curious, and furious people, a woman elbows her way to the front.

For the first time in this chapter of Matthew, we meet a character, a person, who is *not* identified by her place in society. Everyone else has either been introduced by their rank and relation to their community (the tax collector, the Pharisees), or been named as a family member to another person in the story (the father and his daughter). But this woman pushing her way to Jesus is not introduced by her connection to anyone. Instead, she is introduced by a disability. A chronic illness. A secret, private pain: she has been bleeding for *twelve years*. It is strongly implied that she is bleeding from her womb and that because of this bleeding, she either has never had children or has lost many pregnancies. It is strongly implied she is in pain, physically and emotionally and socially, because she is alone and desperate for healing. In a chaotic story where every character is interconnected with the wider story of this region, this town, this synagogue, where we can almost feel the thickness of the crowd pressing in, a woman—this woman—is alone, and she is bleeding.

While everyone is worried about the child who has died, no one seems to be worried about this childless woman. The contrast between the concern for the little girl and the loneliness of this bleeding woman guts me. Everyone is asking Jesus to speak with them, debate them, touch them. This desperate father has asked Jesus to "come and place your hand on her, and she'll live" (Matthew 9:18, CEB).

But this woman skirts around edges and ducks under arms and maybe even shoves someone out of the way so that *she* can touch *Jesus*. She doesn't even ask *him* to touch *her*. Maybe she thinks it's better this way, that he won't notice her, she won't be a burden or a bother. Maybe she doesn't think she's worthy to touch anything but the fraying hem of his robe.

Or maybe she knows exactly what she's doing. Maybe she knows he is the Messiah and knows the story of Isaiah—how in the year King Uzziah died, Isaiah saw the Lord and the hem of the

Lord's robe filled the temple and Isaiah lamented that he was too unworthy to touch even the hem of God's robe (Isaiah 6). And this bleeding woman is full of an audacity that even Isaiah—a prophet!—did not have, because she, a lonely, childless, bleeding woman, reaches out to touch the hem of his robe. She knows just one touch of a fleeting whisper of fabric will *do* something.

So she does it: she darts down and touches the hem of Jesus's robe.

And Jesus *does* notice her. He turns, in the midst of a clamoring crowd, and says to her directly, "Take heart, daughter; your faith has made you well" (Matthew 9:22). We could also translate this from the original Greek as: *Be bold, daughter; your faith has healed you.* Or perhaps *Radiate warmhearted, bolstering courage, daughter; your faith has made you well.*

Jesus sees the woman alone. Jesus sees the woman who is bleeding. Everyone else is worried (rightly, of course) about the little girl who has just died. Jesus, though, sees the childless woman. And Jesus tells her that her audacity to touch him first healed her.

Some of us are pleading, begging Jesus to come and touch us. To heal us. To save the ones we love. And Jesus responds to those pleas, even if it's not in ways we expect or want. But I think some of us could stand to learn from this unnamed, bleeding woman, who has the audacity to reach out first. To touch the hem of his robe.

So often we are taught to be quiet. To accept what we're handed. But to paraphrase Alice Walker's definition of womanism, to follow God is to be audacious. To know that we are beloved even when the world doesn't love us well.

Because Jesus is waiting, encouraging, and telling us: Be bold. Take courage. Your faith—*your* faith—is healing.

. . . .

God our healer;
  we need You to heal us,
  we need You to remember us,
  and we long to touch but the hem of Your robe.
  We know You are our true Physician,
  and we know You never forget us,
  but we need Your help to trust You more.
  You have made us worthy to stand in Your
      courts,
  You have put the crowns on our heads and
      called us Your children.
  Remember us.
  Remind us.
  Amen.

· 23 ·

God Loves Us Bigger

. . . .

Jesus didn't hesitate. He reached down and grabbed
his hand. Then he said, "Faint-heart, what got
into you?"

MATTHEW 14:31 (MSG)

The life-expanding magic of being who God made you to be is not
about being smaller. It is not about letting holiness, or prayer, or
devotion carve you down into half the size you have been. Letting
God love you makes you bigger. Expands you. Pushes the boundaries of what was once considered safe.

Jesus is famed for walking on water, and when he was walking
on the water in the midst of a storm, his friend Peter—bumbling,
foolish, earnest Peter—leapt out of the boat to walk to him. Then,
realizing what he was doing, Peter began to sink. There are a million reasons why he might have done so, but I think at least one
reason was that nagging voice. You know the voice. The voice that
undercuts so many things. The voice that, in this moment for Peter, rose from an undercurrent to a blaring shout: *Who the hell do you
think you are?*

And Peter, facing Jesus, looking straight at the One who made
him and who makes it possible to walk on water, listens to the

voice of self-doubt instead of the voice on the wind over the deep. He panics. He begins to sink. And he cries out: "Lord, save me!" (Matthew 14:30).

Which, of course, Jesus does. And with a gentle reprimand, Jesus says, "You of little faith, why did you doubt?" (Matthew 14:31).

So often this story is interpreted to mean Peter should have trusted Jesus more. And, sure, I think that's likely true. If I trusted Jesus more, I'm certain I would be less anxious and more patient. I'd eat more vegetables and let more people merge in front of me on the highway. Trusting Jesus has nice results.

And Peter had it easy—he was looking right at God doing the thing God was empowering him to do! Imagine if we had the opportunity to do the same!

But . . . don't we? Are we not also looking right at God, doing the thing God has empowered us to do, to be, every time we look in the mirror? And yet, beholding God's beauty in our own reflection, made in the image of God, we lean in and say, *You really just aren't enough.* We're walking on the water, and then we sink.

Trusting Jesus is also about trusting who we are in Christ. Trusting that we are not perfect, we have harmed and been harmed, but we are still worthy of love. We can be forgiven. We can forgive. We can change. We can be bigger and wilder than we ever thought possible.

God will refine us, make no mistake. God will take away our idols, God will challenge us to love more than we think we can. God will rarely ask us to do the easy thing. To quote trans poet and theologian Jay Hulme, "The transcendent truth of who God made us to be can be dangerous in this world." Following God is dangerous because God's enormous love for us and for every single person is enough to overwhelm and threaten every industry and system that profits off of squeezing us down.

Beloveds, be wary of the voices that want you confined and not creative, compliant without capacity to change. To be loved is to be changed, and God will change us. But these changes are carving away what has made us less true, less colorful, less incandescent. Loving God and letting God love you will make you bigger, will expand you. Letting God love you will push the boundaries of what was once considered safe.

But the good news is: God does not love just you, or just me. God loves all of us. And God's desire is for all of us—all of us—to seep and spread into this creation-encompassing abundance. This love that is enough, more than enough, for all of us.

. . . .

God over the waters,
    trouble the current to reveal our course,
    and gentle the foam where we need to
        see clearly.
Help us trust You more,
    in the lines around our eyes
    and the scars in our skin,
    as a blueprint of where You have carried us
        thus far.
Cleave us from the lies that weigh us down,
    and set us free to know:
    there is enough room,
    there is enough love,
    there is enough of You for all of us.
    Amen.

· 24 ·

Baptizing the
Gender-Fringe

. . . .

As they were going along the road, they came to
some water, and the eunuch said, "Look, here is
water! What is to prevent me from being baptized?"
He commanded the chariot to stop, and both of
them, Philip and the eunuch, went down into the
water, and Philip baptized him.

ACTS 8:36, 38

Once again, Jesus is surrounded by a crowd. Old and young. Hopeful and unimpressed. Faithful and furious. Married and blissful,
married and miserable. Queer and heterosexual, gender noncon-
forming and cisgender—but we'll get to that in a moment. The
religious leaders known as Pharisees have once again asked Jesus a
deliberately provocative question—as all good faithful people
ought to do in the presence of God. They ask: *Does the Law (i.e., the
Torah) allow a man to divorce his wife for just any reason?*

Now, our modern ears flinch at the implication that only men
could initiate divorce, but Jewish divorce law was protective of
women compared to the laws of the Roman Empire, which allowed a man to divorce his wife for such reasons as losing her good

looks or not bearing him children or being argumentative. Still, even within a relatively compassionate approach to divorce, if a man divorced a woman, she could be left bereft of resources.

So the sharpness of Jesus's reply to this question is a sharpness aimed at misogyny. He responds: "Haven't you read that at the beginning the creator *made them male and female? And God said, 'Because of this a man should leave his father and mother and be joined together with his wife, and the two will be one flesh.'* So they are no longer two but one flesh. Therefore, humans must not pull apart what God has put together" (Matthew 19:4–6, CEB).

It's a strict answer, stricter than even the Law, and *then* Jesus doubles down, saying: "Not everybody can accept this teaching, but only those who have received the ability to accept it. For there are eunuchs who have been eunuchs from birth. And there are eunuchs who have been made eunuchs by other people. And there are eunuchs who have made themselves eunuchs because of the kingdom of heaven. Those who can accept it should accept it" (Matthew 19:11–12, CEB). This is quite a pivot for Jesus to make. Jesus moves from teaching about the importance of honoring marriage as a lifelong commitment to uplifting eunuchs. Jesus is saying eunuchs are faithful people uniquely positioned to hear what he is saying.

The word *eunuch*, in Jesus's world, encompassed a whole range of people. Some people, through no choice of their own, were made into eunuchs by others because of violent and misogynistic understandings of gender and sexual power. Most famously, eunuchs were people assigned male at birth who were forcibly castrated so that they could serve in royal courts near women without presenting a sexual threat to kings and other men in power. Eunuchs were people excluded from worship (Deuteronomy 23:1) and from the

priesthood (Leviticus 21:20) who experienced acute social alien-
ation for being considered neither male nor female. But *eunuch*
could also refer to someone who chose never to get married to
someone of the opposite sex, someone who consciously chose to
live outside gender norms, or even someone who could not have
biological children.

The biblical conception of eunuchs, then, is a big old category
that has certain parallels with today's categories of gender noncon-
formity or transness or being childfree. It's not a one-to-one
match, and it would be a fool's errand to try to coerce scripture
from two-thousand-plus years ago into our modern norms. But the
point remains: Jesus is talking about what it means for insiders and
outsiders to be in community with each other and, even more so,
in community with God. That remains relevant.

Because he continues to say that, sure, the Law allows room for
divorce, especially in extreme cases, because it was written for
humans, who are "unyielding" and difficult (Matthew 19:8, CEB).
"But," he says, "from the beginning it was not so" (Matthew 19:8).
Meaning: There was no divorce in the Garden of Eden. The Garden where God wove us creatures out of the dust—not out of lack,
not out of need, but out of desire.

So when Jesus is saying in "the beginning it was not so," he's not
listing reasons why people must stay married at all costs. Rather,
Jesus is talking about the original *point* of human connection. He is
saying: *In the beginning, in the Garden, you were made out of my gorgeous
joy, for joy. You were made to be in love with God and each other.*

So when these beloved children of God come to him asking,
How exactly can we force disconnection?, Jesus has a fiery response.
Perhaps part of the fire in Jesus's response is his care for women;
divorce in the ancient world disproportionately harmed women.

But more deeply, Jesus is expressing fiery lament—lament for the shrapnel that cuts when people do not love each other well. It is a primal lament of human disconnection.

And yet: Jesus seems to realize that some people are more likely to understand this divine call to connection and care for each other more than others. Because Jesus has already acknowledged in Matthew 19:11: *Some of y'all are going to get this teaching and some of y'all are not.* And he implies the people who do get this teaching, who *embody* this teaching, are the eunuchs—the people forced to the margins (and the people who are widely considered "unmarriageable") because they don't perfectly fit.

Eunuchs like the Ethiopian eunuch whose story we find in Acts 8.

This story takes place after Jesus's crucifixion and resurrection, when one of his disciples, Philip, has literally been carried by God into the wilderness outside Jerusalem. There he encounters a government official visiting from Ethiopia who is a triple-outsider: a non-Jewish, African eunuch. And to Philip's shock, this non-Jewish, African eunuch is reading the book of Isaiah, a text sacred to followers of God. So Philip asks, "Do you understand what you are reading?" (Acts 8:30). And the eunuch replies, "How can I, unless someone guides me?" (Acts 8:31). And so the eunuch, whom Christian tradition has given the name "Simeon Bachos," invites Philip into the chariot he's sitting in.

Did you catch that? Simeon Bachos, the triple-outsider, *welcomes Philip into his chariot.* This proto-queer person welcomes the proto-Christian evangelist into his sacred, cool, safe space.

And after Simeon and Philip talk for a while and Simeon learns about Jesus, Simeon turns and says to Philip, "Look, here is water! What is to prevent me from being baptized?" (Acts 8:36). What is to prevent me from being baptized? What is to stop me from choosing to know the love of God, to die and rise with Christ, to be counted among the Body of Christ as hands and feet of Jesus in this world?

What is going to block our access to the God of the universe, who cast the stars in their courses and had the brilliance to teach cells to divide in order to multiply? Who is going to stand in the way of the God who has counted each hair on our heads?

No one. No one gets to do that.

Because this love has always been for *all* of us. From the Garden where two earth-creatures were hewn from clay to the end of time when we are all wrapped up in the tender arms of a God who has always loved us as a Mother. The love of God is for all of us. Those whom God has woven together from the clay, let no one tear asunder.

....

Creator of the dust,
    and the One who dusts us off when we are
        pushed down,
  we have been hurt.
  We have hurt others.
  We need Your love to fold in the fringes,
  to circle the center of our beings
  and our hearts and our communities,
  where we know Your love already is,
  but we need to see it. Feel it.
  More.
  For how much more You have made us than for
    division.

For how much more You have made us than for
    harm.
For how much more You have woven creation.

Help us be more.
    Help us trust the *more* within us.
    Help us know You are more than we could ever
        imagine or hope for.
    We know You can, and You will, and You are,
        and You have done.
    Amen.

25

A God You Can Kick
in the Shins

....

When Mary reached the place where Jesus was and
saw him, she fell at his feet and said, "Lord, if you
had been here, my brother would not have died."
When Jesus saw her weeping . . . he was deeply
moved in spirit and troubled. . . . Jesus wept.

JOHN 11:32–33, 35 (NIV)

Mary and Martha are the first women in the Gospel of John to say
to Jesus: *You* are the Messiah, the Son of God, the One coming into
the world. They are the first to know who Jesus is. Before Peter,
before the Beloved Disciple, before anyone else, these women
know who God is in Jesus. But they proclaim this in a moment not
of great joy but of unutterable agony. A moment when they feel
that Jesus Christ, Son of God, had abandoned them. Which means
the first person in the Gospel of John to know that Jesus is the Son
of God, the Messiah, is a woman who is screaming at him.

Mary and Martha were two of Jesus's best friends. His ride-or-
die people. When so many of the stories about Jesus see him en-
meshed in a thick, needy crowd, the stories that include Mary and
Martha always have a cool timbre to them. Like their home was

his quiet retreat, a place where he was loved and tended to. A place where he could let his hair down.

And then: Mary and Martha's brother, Lazarus, got sick. Jesus heard through the grapevine that Lazarus was ill, but he didn't make it in time to say goodbye before Lazarus died. *Days* later, as Jesus is *finally* making his way to their home—a place where he spent so many happy hours with Martha and Mary and Lazarus— the sisters come running out to him and say, "Lord, if you had been here, my brother would not have died" (John 11:21, 32). They are angry. They are furious. They feel betrayed and confused and lost and guilty. Mostly, I think, they are sad.

And, instead of offering them a lecture on how to be faithful, instead of admonishing them for being sad or angry, Jesus weeps. It is the shortest but perhaps most profound verse in the whole Bible: "Jesus wept" (John 11:35, NIV). Jesus crawls down into the hole of their sorrow, and he cries with them. Mourns with them. Laments with them.

I never thought this verse would matter so much to me. And then four people in my family blew up in a tragic, unexplained plane engine malfunction in Alaska. They were killed instantly, along with their best friends with whom they were vacationing. My father had to track down their family dentist to get their dental records in order to identify the bodies. They were shipped to us, all four of them, in a box no bigger than a pair of shoes. My father cradled them in his arms, the sole pallbearer, as he laid them in the soft earth.

One of the worst parts—at least, in the blur of those early days of shock and fury—was how much news coverage there was. Everywhere we went on the church campus as we planned and then attended their funerals, there were cameras. I knew in some distant, rational part of my brain that this was because many, many people were grieving their loss. Nine people from the same town, the same church, five kids from the same school, had died in a freak accident. But when the reporters were calling my freshly divorced mother for her "comments" on the "tragedy," I wanted to rip their cameras apart piece by cold metallic piece.

My father, though, through some combination of internal strength, autopilot, and a need to speak, agreed to make a statement to their flashing lenses and quiet voices after the first of so many funerals. I can't remember if they asked about his faith, or if he was prepared with a statement, but as he held my hand, he looked right into the camera and said, "We know God did not do this to us; we know, as it says in John 11, that Jesus is weeping with us."

Jesus wept.

And in so doing, Jesus showed us that it is okay to be angry with God. It is okay to be disappointed in God, *especially* when we are in the vortex of grief.

The year after my family members died, there are whole weeks I remember with caustic clarity, like the lights were too bright. And then there are weeks, months, that seem to fade into a colorless blur. But somewhere in there, I remember a specific class with my favorite professor, Jane Crosthwaite, during my last year of college at Mount Holyoke. We were reading Phyllis Trible's *Texts of Terror*, a book about the worst, most sexually violent stories in the Bible. I don't remember, exactly, what Jane had asked, but it was something to the effect of: Why *do we still read these stories? What do we do with them? How could those of us who believe in God still believe in God after . . . this?*

The room was silent. And that's when she cleared her throat

and, in a North Carolina drawl that had not ceded an inch to the Massachusetts winter, said, "You don't want a God you can't kick in the shins."

Jesus shows us that God doesn't want us to have a God we can't kick in the shins. Jesus shows us that sometimes the *most* faithful thing we can do is yell at God. Scream at God. Hurl the worst insults we can: *If you were real, this would not have happened. If you cared, this would not have happened. If you had been here, he would not have died!*

God is big enough to take it. God is holy enough and powerful enough that our anger does not diminish our faith—it is the deepest cry of faith we can speak.

....

God,
>sometimes it feels like You have just walked
>away,
>leaving us squalling in our basket,
>begging for You to cradle us, carry us home.
>We are hurt. We are angry. We can't believe You
>would do this to us.
>Help us see.
>Help us trust.
>And if nothing else—weep with us.
>We know You do.
>Or, at least, we're trying.
>Amen.

26

A Drag Queen Messiah

. . . .

Say to Daughter Zion, "Look, your king is coming
to you, humble and riding on a donkey, and on a
colt the donkey's offspring."

MATTHEW 21:5 (CEB)

Why did Jesus die? Why was he executed as a criminal when even
the governor himself said he could find no crime? Why was God
incarnate pierced in the side by soldiers who tormented him,
mourned by women who could do nothing to stop his pain?

No one devotional can encapsulate why. No *lifetime* of sermons
or Bible studies or prayer can "solve" the mystery of why the Living God decided to submit to a brutal human execution. Because
to love God is to love a holy mystery, and on some level, the death
of Jesus remains a mystery. To paraphrase theologian Fleming Rutledge: no other major world religion has a dead god at its center.
But we do.

And it is inexplicable, incomprehensible—but that hasn't
stopped us from trying to understand, practically, why this happened. Because we can behold the execution of Jesus and see sinfulness at work. We can see the ways we still put people on our
own versions of the cross to bear the sins of our own violence and

hatred. The lethal injection gurney is shaped like a cross. Michael Brown, lying on the street in Ferguson, Missouri, died with his arms out. George Floyd cried out for his mama. Sandra Bland was killed without trial. As Rev. James Cone hauntingly illuminates in his book *The Cross and the Lynching Tree*, the way white supremacy in the United States works, and has worked, is in direct parallel to the powers and principalities of evil and empire that put Christ on the cross. Jesus Christ was a racial minority lynched to appease the brutal hunger of an empire who demanded sacrifices to their favorite god: themselves.

But . . . why? What was the threat?

Jesus's entry into Jerusalem is a clear and definitive moment when Jesus did *something* that made the empire angry enough to kill him. He did something to make his community afraid that his actions would bring pain upon all of them. To understand what, exactly, Jesus did to make the empire so angry, we have to understand what was happening in Jerusalem historically at the same time as this Palm Sunday processional.

In the ancient world, conquering armies seized cities and maintained their power by parades and shows of might through the defeated city. Occupying armies could roll up to a place they had subjugated with all their muscle and might, flex their power in a parade, and maybe rough up a few onlookers as a reminder that they were judge and jury, the law of the land.

Theologians Marcus Borg and John Dominic Crossan have argued this is exactly what was happening in Jerusalem on Palm Sunday. Pontius Pilate and his cronies have come to town *because* it is Passover, a time when the Jews remembered they had defeated an empire—Egypt—before. As he entered the city, Borg and Crossan write, "Pilate's procession displayed not only imperial power, but also Roman imperial theology. According to this theology, the emperor was not simply the ruler of Rome, but the Son of God. It began with the greatest of the emperors, Augustus, who ruled Rome from 31 BCE to 14 CE." Pilate was no fool. He was there to make sure no one got any ideas about freedom, and to remind people who the Son of God really was: Caesar. Empires thrive on forced forgetfulness. Empires thrive on banning books, erasing the stories of freedom.

But while Pilate enters from the west, Jesus enters from the east. While Pilate parades into the city in a show of masculine military might, Jesus is riding the most non-militaristic mount that could be: a nursing donkey and her wee little colt scampering beside her. (In some Gospels, Jesus rides on the colt, not the mother—and yet the tender image of a nursing child remains.) Jesus, our Mother Hen, is the one who will set people *free* from empire. And the people are so wild and desperate and hungry and delighted to see this Messiah that they start ripping branches off of trees to shade his head and tearing clothes from their bodies to form a makeshift carpet on which he might tread. There is no military parade, no show of arms, nothing but skin and leaves and a mother donkey with her baby and this bizarre, gentle rabbi.

To quote theologian Debie Thomas, "As Pilate clanged and crashed his imperial way into Jerusalem from the west, Jesus approached from the east, looking (by contrast) ragtag and absurd. His was the procession of the ridiculous, the powerless, the explicitly vulnerable." Jesus's so-called triumphal entry into Jerusalem was a deliberate subversion of imperial power. From the donkey to the people tearing off their clothes with shouts of "Hosanna!," Jesus is making a mockery of the great show of the Roman emperor's "Son of God" power by actually being the Son of God.

And to me? Jesus's entry into Jerusalem was not unlike that of a drag queen.

Drag is a performance art form that takes the bizarre and banal to an extreme, holding up a mirror to our lives so we can find humor and release in the silliness of being alive. Drag uses bold makeup and exaggerated dance moves to illumine ludicrous beauty standards and at the same time uplift what is beautiful in the mundane reality of life. Drag is an art form rooted in protest, in unraveling gender roles, and in unspooling militaristic masculinity through femininity. As drag artist Sasha Velour says, the art of drag is able to "create something new in the mixing of seeming opposites." Drag uses artifice to show us what is artificial about power in our world.

In that sense, Jesus's entrance sounds an awful lot like the art of drag. New Creation takes the tools of conquest and might and laughs at them in the face of the gentleness of God's almighty power. His costume is a bold *lack* of armor or military might. He does not need swords or armies for his power. He knows these powers of empire will kill him. And yet there he sits, on a donkey, laughing at the devil with a few palm leaves as improvised, earnest props and a crowd of hungry, desperate, freedom-seeking people.

And as Jesus marches by sitting, and conquers by submitting, and wears the simple robes of a poor peasant, the people begin to scream "Hosanna!," which means "Save us!"

God *save* us. Because we don't have to do a lot of imagining to see how being a drag queen is still a threat to empire. We don't have to do a lot of imagining to see how a ragtag group of people seeking joy are classified as a threat to heavily armed battalions. We do not have to do much imagining to see how our tender, effeminate, soft God died. It happened two thousand years ago, but what we long for remains the same: *Save us, God. Save us.*

. . . .

Holy God,
    Holy and Mighty,
    Holy Immortal One,
    have mercy on us.
    You are the true king,
    crowned on Your nursing donkey and her colt,
    triumphant in tenderness.

We too often bow to kings and powers of
        this world
    that enshrine vengeance instead of mercy,
    anger instead of compassion,
    conquest instead of obedience to You.
    We ask for Your forgiveness.

Save us.
    Save us.
    Save us!

Holy God,
    Holy and Mighty,
    Holy Immortal One,
    have mercy on us.

Amen.

27

Judas Got His Feet
Washed, Too

....

Having loved his own who were in the world, he
loved them to the end. . . . He poured water into a
basin and began to wash the disciples' feet and to
wipe them with the towel that was tied around him.

JOHN 13:1, 5

Mere hours before Jesus Christ is publicly executed by the empire
on a cross, Jesus gathers with his friends for what we now call
the Last Supper. John 13:1 starts this scene with the words "Having loved his own who were in the world, he loved them to the
end." And Judas, the traitor, is there, as one of "his own"—Jesus's
own.

Sometimes, the commandment to "love your neighbor" and the
commandment to "love your enemy" are the same thing. I used to
think "loving my enemies" meant loving people who were threatening to me because they were scary strangers—out there, far off.
But then I experienced betrayals by friends, by family. And I
learned that loving someone does not stop them from being an
enemy sometimes. Harder still: being an enemy does not make
someone beyond love.

Judas was Jesus's friend. Judas had already gone to the religious leaders who were afraid of what wrath Jesus would bring upon their people with his anti-government actions. He had profited, richly, from selling out Jesus. Yet there he was. "His own."

John's Gospel is the only one to make a real point of Judas's presence in this sacrificial love offering by Jesus. John's Gospel is also the only one to show Jesus washing the feet of the disciples. Jesus strips off his outer clothes, wraps himself in a towel that he will use to wipe their feet, kneels at the feet of his friends and his enemies, and cleans them. This is as vulnerable, and intimate, and scandalous as you can imagine. Not a week prior, Mary washed Jesus's feet with pure nard, an *extremely* expensive perfume, in an act of tender worship and knowledge—knowledge that Jesus would die, that she would need this perfume to honor him in his burial (John 12:7). Judas lambasted Mary for such an inexcusably frivolous use of money. And now Jesus is washing Judas's feet, knowing that Judas is the one who will betray him.

I do not know why Judas betrays Jesus. Christians have squabbled over this for millennia. The Common English Bible translates John 13:2 as "the devil had already provoked Judas," whereas the New Revised Standard Version Updated Edition offers "the devil had already decided" or, in the footnotes, "put it into his heart." Our imagination of this devil is likely more informed by literary biblical fanfiction (Dante, Milton, et al.) than by the Bible itself, but even in a theological worldview that sees the devil as *almost* as powerful as God, we ought to know that, even now, in this moment before Jesus dies, the devil is not ultimately in charge. Judas might be a pawn, someone lost to his own temptations and the greater machinations of people seeking power while under threat, but Judas is not without agency.

And still, Jesus washes Judas's feet.

I wonder what the disciples said hours later about Jesus washing Judas's feet, as they hid from the Roman soldiers, or when they huddled in locked rooms after the crucifixion, or when the women prepared the nard again to anoint Jesus's body. Were they hurt that Jesus offered such tenderness to the traitor? Did they feel betrayed that Jesus let such scum be included? Did they think, in moments of desperate anger, that Jesus deserved what was coming because of his effeminate tolerance of Judas?

Because Jesus's mercy is outright offensive. To our most self-protective impulses, to our most revolutionary dreams, the mercy of Jesus Christ is not sensible, clever, or digestible. Mercy is rarely palatable. And I don't think Jesus intends for mercy to be palatable—but we want digestible grace.

I think that's why we're so bad at talking about forgiveness and mercy. So many Christians have wielded forced forgiveness as a weapon, telling the abused to forgive their abusers and even return to keep enduring that abuse. But Jesus does not wash Judas's feet and then remain silent about the harm Judas has caused. As Archbishop Desmond Tutu wrote, "In forgiving, people are not being asked to forget." Jesus tells the truth about his betrayal. And when we rush past the truth-telling part of reconciliation to fake "forgiveness," we are not truly forgiving—we are concealing harm for the sake of silence in the name of peace. We are asking people to be Jesus instead of letting Jesus be Jesus. Because the actual power of forgiveness is saying: *Something wrong, something bad, happened here.* We don't forgive good things.

That Jesus freely chooses to wash Judas's feet is what makes him truly merciful. And as offensive as Jesus Christ's mercy is, it is a liberative act of grace and care that says: *Even now, even with all*

*you have done and will do, you are still welcome. Still wanted. Still loved
as a friend, as my own, to the end.*

No one is beyond the mercy of God. Even Judas was given this
mercy. Even Judas's feet were washed by the friend whom he
wanted gone.

I think the act of washing Judas's feet can teach us why mercy
is so important even as it is wildly unpopular. Because we have
all harmed, betrayed, and hurt people, perhaps beyond what we
could even comprehend. And we have all been harmed, perhaps in
ways that we cannot even fully articulate. I suspect, from years of
pastorally walking alongside people, that all of us have been a
Judas, at least once. And all of us have had a Judas betray us, at
least once.

We are not always able to offer mercy the way Jesus did. Jesus
is, after all, truly God and truly human. Sometimes, we do offer
mercy and it's just not received. Judas did not receive the fullness
of mercy.

But to the end, Jesus loved him, his own. I wonder: What do
you need to be free of to receive mercy? What do you need to be
set free from to extend mercy? What mercy is yours to give, and
what mercy do you need Jesus to offer?

. . . .

Holy God, heavenly Father,
     You formed us from the dust in Your image
          and likeness,
     You washed the feet of Your friends
          and enemies,
     showing the way of mercy,

and You stand ready to wash us clean of what
    has been done to us,
and the harm we have done to others.
Free us from the chains of sin.
Free us from the haunting of harm.
Show us what we need to live into Your mercy.
In the name of God, Father, Son, and Holy
    Spirit,
Amen.

· 28 ·

Breastfeeding the Body of Christ

. . . .

While they were eating, Jesus took a loaf of bread, and after blessing it he broke it, gave it to the disciples, and said, "Take, eat; this is my body."

MATTHEW 26:26

*As a mother comforts her child,
so I will comfort you.*

ISAIAH 66:13

They say you are what you eat. Which means when we eat the body and blood of Jesus Christ, we are the body of Jesus Christ.

This is what I was taught in catechism as a child in Catholic Sunday school. As I prepared for my first Communion, I'm sure I had questions—lots of them—but what I remember feeling mostly was an overwhelming sense of calm. I imagined heaven (in the cloudy sky, naturally) peppered with angels and a giant Jesus, like one of those inflatable figures you see on lawns at Christmastime. And Jesus was absolutely bedotted with tiny, perfectly round, Communion-wafer-sized holes.

Because we had eaten him, of course. That's why he had to be so big. Because lots of people, for lots of years, had eaten Jesus.

I am *certain* my Communion teachers had *not* told me this exact picture was what to expect; my little imagination had done plenty of its own theological work.

Incidentally, I think a lot of parents feel a lot of anxiety about weirding out their kids when it comes to religion, or fear that introducing children to faith is inherently indoctrinating them without agency. Trust me, Communion is no weirder than talking blue heelers who teach gentle parenting in twenty-minute segments, or a boy who got bit by a spider and now is part man, part arachnid. Communion is definitely less weird than first heartbreaks, those moments when our children first learn what unjust pain feels like. It is less mystifying, in some ways, than children suffering from cancer. Or parents who have cancer and will leave their children all too soon.

Life is weird and hard to understand. Sometimes we need an anchor that is also weird and hard to understand.

Equipping children with the rituals of life and death that have persisted for millennia does not mean they will always, or even ever, believe in God. It means we are offering them a place to make some sense of an often senseless world through the great and ancient art of stories. *Eucharist* is just the Greek word for "giving of thanks," and as with any good meal, it is when we give thanks to God for everything God gives us . . . including God.

And, y'all, I know: the Eucharist is *weird*. Every week I stand behind a table and say: *Here is our God who died. And rose again. And is coming back. Let's eat Him.*

Trying to sanitize or explain this in palatable terms is impossible. But as a child, this just made sense to me as one more weird and holy thing in a world of weird and holy things. We grown-ups forget: children have no real sense of what is "normal" except what we equip them with and what their intuition can devise. If I told my toddler we went into space and landed on another planet when we visit Auntie Brenna, she would believe me—and it would be no stranger than the truth that humans have sent astronauts to the moon and taken pictures of distant planets.

So why not tell her the truth? God gives us God's own body to eat.

And honestly, it's not as strange as it sounds. Because here's the thing that I didn't even realize until I was pregnant: my baby *ate my flesh* for almost three years—the nine months I carried her, when my entire body created and sustained her entire body, and the two years she enthusiastically nursed on, as she called it, "mama boob."

All of us—*all of us*—only got here because we feasted on someone else's blood. Whether we know her or not, our birth mother's body sustained us. Fed us. From her own body. And after birth, if the birthing person can and chooses to do so, babies are sustained by breastmilk. For centuries before the genuine miracle of formula, the human population only survived because people fed babies with their bodies.

Breastmilk is blood made into food for an infant child to eat. And not just any food—in the words of writer and speaker Angela Garbes, contact with the baby's saliva lets the nursing person's "body produce . . . the specific antibodies needed to quell the infection," essentially "tailor-mak[ing] medicine . . . like a kind of compound pharmacy." When my daughter had to be transported via ambulance to the hospital after contracting RSV, the nurses said the best thing I could do was breastfeed her, because my very body was going to help her fight. My body was going to make medicine for my child who was so sick she needed to be on oxygen for a week.

Do you know what magic that was to me, as a mother, helplessly watching my child struggle to breathe? She is my heart outside of my body. I had no choice but to seek help, and that help told me that my own body would make blood into food customized for my sick child's healing. I did already know this, but to hear it in that moment from a professional was a gift from God. My body was her sanctuary even as she lived outside of it. My mere breathing protected her. What a God-given gift.

And, knowing this ancient and weird and holy way life has always sustained us, does it not make perfect sense that this is how the Mother of us all, Jesus Christ, feeds us? Loves us? As the hour of death came, the King of Heaven, Jesus Christ, did the first thing his mother did for him after giving birth in that stable: he offered his beloved children sustenance from his own body. Just as mothers and wet nurses and nannies have done for millennia to keep the human race alive, Jesus Christ offered his very body for food.

. . . .

Life-giving God:
    You gather us around Your table,
    and say: That's good.
    You give Your body for our food,
    and say: That's good.
    Thank You for feeding us in these
      holy mysteries,

nourish us with what we need to love and
   serve You
in ourselves, in each other, and in this world
   You have created
through Your Son, Jesus Christ,
by whom and with whom and in whom,
in the unity of the Holy Spirit,
all honor and glory and praise are Yours,
   forevermore.
Amen.

29

God's Own Body

....

For as the body is clad in the cloth, and the flesh in
the skin, and the bones in the flesh, and the heart
in the chest, so are we, soul and body, clad in the
goodness of God and enclosed in it. . . . There is no
being made that can know how much and how
sweetly and how tenderly our Maker loves us.

SAINT JULIAN OF NORWICH,
REVELATIONS OF DIVINE LOVE

Breastfeeding my child was a wonder of my body, a gift of life and
comfort and sanctuary to us both for nearly two years.

And breastfeeding was hell on earth for me.

My body was a wonderland. My body was a traitor. Because
while my body did this Eucharistic magic of transforming my
blood into food for my child, at about three months in, breastfeeding began to hurt like the flames of the inferno. I'm not exaggerat-
ing when I say I would have rather given birth again. No one could
figure out why I was in such agony. I saw breast specialists and
oncologists and lactation consultants and even emergency room
doctors when the mastitis had me borderline delusional with pain.
I was on ten different kinds of antibiotics. Nothing helped.

And my daughter would not—would *not*—take a bottle. Don't

bother telling me your incredible trick for getting your perfect child to take a bottle. Whatever it is, we tried it. We tried them all. None of them worked. She inherited my iron will, I suppose.

So I fed her, bleeding, ten times a day, for months. And months. My husband would hold my hand, or rub my feet, all while steadily reading aloud from novels while I clenched a leather belt between my teeth. I sent my soul outside of my body. I did hypno-breathing. Sometimes, I screamed until my throat was raw. I broke my own body to feed my body to her because there is nothing, *nothing* I would not do for her.

And: I felt like I had no other choice. This was not a freely given gift as much as I want to believe of myself it was. It was love—ferocious love, self-sacrificial love. But it had a *cost*.

Over and over and over I prayed, *This is my body, broken for you.* Not because I ever had the notion I was Jesus, but because Jesus was saving me in that moment. I grasped the most infinitesimal amount of what it meant for God to break open God's own body for us, because I did it, for a finite time, for my one child. Jesus carried me through that pain. I could not have done it without him.

And as much as this devotional is here to offer you holy mysteries and unravel simplistic theology, I want to say, from the guts of my prayers to you, don't be afraid to plead the blood of Jesus. I was there on my knees begging Jesus to save me, *save me* from this pain.

And then an angel appeared: a nurse practitioner who figured out I had a staph infection on my skin that was flaring chronic mastitis, both of which caused me this unbearable pain. She prescribed me a ten-dollar over-the-counter antiseptic body cleanser.

I felt better by the end of the next day. May God give her a lifetime of perfectly cool pillows and the best parking spots everywhere she goes.

I was granted an honest-to-God miracle. When it came time for me to wean, it was *my* choice. That mattered acutely to me: that I could make a choice out of my own desire and not out of desperation. My body could be mine again.

And this is how God is God and I am not: God continually, forever, gives us God's own body. God *gives us* God's *own body*. And, yes, this is a profoundly feminine action. But it is subversive and revolutionary not "just" because of the connections between nursing bodies and our Heavenly Mother who holds us to her breast. God giving us God's own body is also revolutionary because God knows we must eat, and God takes the place of an animal meant to be eaten.

In Jesus's day, people in many different religions were always making sacrifices to gods. In first-century Judaism, God had commanded animal sacrifices be made. To be clear, these animals were not just killed and then left to rot. While the blood was burned as the offering, the meat of these animal sacrifices *was eaten*, some by the people providing the sacrifice and some by the clergy performing the sacrifice, as payment for their services.* It was a holy barbecue. It's not *that* different from saying grace before dinner, if you eat animals. And that's kind of what these sacrifices acknowledged: we depend on creation for our life, so we give back to God what God gave to us.

---

* I will accept excellent cuts of brisket should any of my parishioners like to bring this practice back.

And God had made provision for people of all economic stand-ings to make animal sacrifices, even if they didn't have much money; in Luke 2:24, when the infant Jesus is presented at the temple, Mary and Joseph make an economy offering of two turtledoves or pigeons. But then, some thirty years after his fam-ily makes that sacrifice on his behalf, Jesus, true God and true human, breaks bread and pours wine and says: *Take, eat, this is my body, given for you. Drink this, all of you, for this is my blood of the new covenant.*

The revelation of this revolution is that no one has to be the sacrifice, not even the wee little pigeons. *God* does the God-sacrifice. Because only God can give endlessly out of endless life. God will give God's own body for our life, because no one else actually can. As healing and magical as it was to breastfeed my daughter, I cannot protect her from all harm. That is not failure, it is a condition of me being human. My body cannot always house or feed my child. It just can't. But God's can.

Partaking in the Holy Eucharist, this feast of God's flesh, is not some magical elixir we eat to bulletproof ourselves from pain, vi-olence, or death. But it is the means of death made into life by the source of life—God. The One whom we nourish ourselves on, who made our mothers and will make our children. The One who made us feeds us in a way our mothers never fully could, in ways we can never fully do for our children or for ourselves.

This is why it matters to me that God does the God-sacrifice: It is not about God demanding a sacrifice for vengeance, or blood-lust, or hunger. It is about God saying, *Where you are incomplete, or unable, or too weak, or too scared, I will go. I will feed you. I will be what you cannot be for yourself but desperately need.*

. . . .

God, who wraps us in Your care,
    clasping us to Your breast,
    giving us what we long for most—

Thank You for feeding us with the spiritual food of
        Your body and blood.
    Thank You for knowing what we need before
            we can ever utter a word.
    Thank You for being there in the stark ache of
        our souls,
    in the gnaw of our hunger.

Thank You for loving us so completely.

We ask that You soothe us where we are struggling,
    fill us where we feel empty,
    and remind us:
    we are small
    and held
    in the eternal cradle of Your arms.

Amen.

30

The Cross Was a Weapon

. . . .

It was now about noon, and darkness came over
the whole land until three in the afternoon, while
the sun's light failed, and the curtain of the temple
was torn in two. Then Jesus, crying out with a loud
voice, said, "Father, into your hands I commend my
spirit." Having said this, he breathed his last.

LUKE 23:44–46

Within toxic theologies that claim God hates us, Jesus's death on
the cross has often been used as *the* pinnacle reason. The cross is
the place where God's wrath was satisfied, say these theologies.
It's almost like the suffering Christ is staring us down, saying,
Look at what you made me do. Anyone who doesn't believe this is
said to be engaging in wishful thinking to avoid a challenging
truth. But the real challenge is to behold the trauma, and loss, and
death on the cross *while also* beholding Christ's love and solidarity
with us.

So let's be clear about the reality of the cross. In ancient Rome,
the cross was a weapon of war. Crucifixion in Jesus's day was a
means of execution reserved, with few exceptions, for foreigners
or non-citizens of Rome, and to suppress slave revolts. Crucifixion
was deliberately public, slow torture meant to demonstrate the

empire's might. Crucified people died from exposure, the beatings that often came before being crucified, and from a slow drowning in their own bodily fluids.

One of the most bizarre things we do as Christians is to adore, even revere, the weapon that killed Jesus. As Rev. Dr. James Cone, one of the greatest theologians of the past century, writes, "The cross has been transformed into a harmless, non-offensive ornament that Christians wear around their necks." We've become so inoculated against the brutality of what the cross symbolized in the ancient world that we don't see it as shocking.

Wearing a cross on a necklace, for a first-century person, would be like me wearing a necklace with a silver filigreed AK-47 or drone. I'm not saying the cross is not a powerful or beautiful thing for us to wear or behold with adoration—I'm simply saying we need to be conscious of what we are doing. If we wear a weapon, it should be to say that death has lost its sting. We should not wear a cross necklace or have a cross tattoo to wield the weapon that killed Jesus as a weapon against other people.

So how do we see the cross for what it really was? For this, I turn to Cone's brilliant book *The Cross and the Lynching Tree*, which argues that Jesus's crucifixion was a first-century lynching. Jesus was lynched in the sense that, historically, Jesus's death mirrors the lynchings of Black people, other people of color, and perceived dissidents across America: it was an unjust, mob-mentality-driven, extralegal killing, carried out under the boot of empire. And also, Jesus was lynched in the sense that whenever a member of the Body of Christ dies an unjust, brutal death, this pain is being inflicted *in* and *on* Christ.

"The cross needs the lynching tree," Cone writes, "to remind Americans of the reality of suffering—to keep the cross from

becoming a symbol of abstract, sentimental piety. Before the spectacle of the cross we are called to more than contemplation and
adoration. We are faced with a clear challenge: as Latin American liberation theologian Jon Sobrino has put it, 'to take the
crucified down from the cross.'" When we stand and behold the
death of our Savior on a tree, we see everyone else ever crucified
as well.

In the lynchings of the Jim Crow era and the lynchings of today. When children are starving and their parents have been
bombed and the doctors have nothing but vinegar to treat wounds.
When families are forced to leave everything they knew and travel
for miles with nothing but holes in their shoes and hope for a more
hospitable welcome in a land where there are razor-wire buoys in
the rivers. In the silenced anguish of family members or supposed
friends sexually abusing children. In the ravages of the unspeakable harm we do to each other by our own fault, or by our inaction,
or by our willful ignorance.

Jesus saves us on and from the cross *not* because the Father has
to mete out some almighty punishment to make you personally
feel bad but because we live in a world *full* of crucifixion.

When I see the crucifixions still ongoing in this world, it actually starts to make sense that Jesus died in this gruesome, horrify-
ing way. Because God is saying, *There is nowhere you can go, nothing
you can endure, that I do not know. That I do not understand. That I have
not also endured.* The things we find unspeakable? The traumas too
horrific for us to face in our newsfeeds or in our own lives? God
went there. To the unspeakable, haunting, horrific place.

Because *only* God can bear this. So often I hear well-meaning
Christians value standing in "the middle," like Jesus did. Reaching

out to "both sides," being friends to enemies and friends alike. This is absolutely our work to do and what Jesus asks us to do. But we are kidding ourselves if we don't see that *only* Jesus can *actually* do this in complex completeness.

Jesus hung on the cross with his arms extended to the people who betrayed and lynched him, to those lynched *with* him, and to the women who stayed with him. Jesus loves the victim and the victimizer, and it was this posture of his arms being extended on the cross *that killed him* by drowning him in his own blood. "Father, forgive them," he says with labored breath. Jesus, with his arms outstretched to either side, is the only one who can truly sacrifice the whole of himself for our pain to bear it. He can reach the victimizer and the victim and love them both, and *that love will drown him*. But it will not defeat him.

And Jesus was not obligated to do this; our God *chose* to do this. Only God can endure such suffering from a place of total love and total freedom of choice. Our God was willing to suffer out of love, not hatred.

And only God can endure crucifixion and live. And it is only by the grace of God that we can face the crucifixions of our lives, and our world. Because even from the cross, from the pit of death, Jesus says: *I know what you have lost, what you have faced, what you grieve down to the bones of the earth and up to the stars in their courses, and I will never, ever let you face it alone.*

. . . .

Lord Jesus Christ,
    Son of the living God,
    You are the Savior of the world,

and You hung on that tree,
   for us.

For us.

Save us and help us,
   we humbly plead You.

Be with us, now,
   and at the hour of our death.
   Amen.

You Will Know Him
by Broken Bread

....

When he was at the table with them, he took bread,
blessed and broke it, and gave it to them.

LUKE 24:30

The risen Christ appears first to women, in all four Gospels. These
women tell their fellow disciples—but most of the men hear their
words as "nonsense" (Luke 24:11, CEB). Luke 24 tells the story of
two of these people who loved Jesus. They're fleeing Jerusalem for
a village called Emmaus, because while the reality of the world
has been upended in the resurrection of Christ, the reality of the
Roman Empire remains a threat. Their feet are heavy. Their hearts
are heavy. Their minds are muddled; these crazy women have told
them a crazy story about Jesus being raised from the dead.

And then Jesus appears before them—but they're "prevented
from recognizing him" (Luke 24:16, CEB). They think he's just another traveler on the road. In one of the Bible's best ironies, Jesus
asks them what they're talking about. And with "their faces
downcast," these two friends stop in the middle of the road
(Luke 24:17, CEB). One of them asks Jesus—utterly bewildered, if
not a little angry—"Are you the only visitor to Jerusalem who is

unaware of the things that have taken place there over the last few days?" (Luke 24:18, CEB).

I can't help but imagine Jesus has a little teasing smile as he responds, "What things?" (Luke 24:19, CEB). And they respond— again, the irony!—by telling Jesus about his own crucifixion. But then, they continue, "There's more: Some women from our group have left us stunned. They went to the tomb early this morning and didn't find his body. They came to us saying that they had even seen a vision of angels who told them he is alive. Some of those who were with us went to the tomb and found things just as the women said. They didn't see him" (Luke 24:22–24, CEB).

And to this tidy little monologue of woe and confusion about disbelieving the women who are the first preachers of Christ's resurrection, Jesus responds with the ever compassionate: "You foolish people!" (Luke 24:25, CEB). Now, maybe Jesus's tone was chiding. Even a little condescending. But I think most of the time, when God calls us mortals foolish, it's less like "You stupid morons" and more like "You silly goose!" *Silly goose! The Messiah told you he'd be back! Don't you remember?*

And then—this is where it gets really fascinating to me—the book of Luke just gives a summary: "Then beginning with Moses and all the prophets, he interpreted to them the things about himself in all the scriptures" (Luke 24:27). That's all. We don't get an itemized list of things Jesus says the disciples need to believe. There is no moment in which they say a particular prayer, a statement of faith, or a confession of sin for abandoning him. No. We just get one sentence summarizing Jesus's interpretation of the scriptures.

I suspect part of why we don't get a specific list of things Jesus wants these disciples to know and believe is that he's interpreting the scriptures for *them* personally. We, the audience of this story, are outsiders to the counsel Jesus offered to his friends in a moment of trauma. We only get a summary. And that is actually really powerful to me, because I think this moment is a kind of antidote to one-size-fits-all theology, to clichés like "God won't give you more than you can handle" or "Your suffering is for God's glory" or "Everything happens for a reason." Jesus does not dictate phrases we Christians can say (with the best of intentions and yet often with negative consequences). Jesus does not offer a platitude; he walks alongside his traumatized friends.

Because here's the thing about platitudes: there have been times of suffering in my life when I encountered proclamations like "God's punishments are also God's blessings" and they actually felt really true to me—in part because these came from other people telling their own stories of making sense of their losses, rather than people prescribing a response to me. They felt life-giving and resonant and full. But I have also endured losses that did *not* feel like divine punishment as blessing, and when people tried to say things like that to me, it only increased my pain. Context was key, because rarely is there a one-size-fits-all theological interpretation of any given situation.

This does not mean that our relationship with God is some kind of bespoke service, offered up on a platter for our individual consumption without connection to a greater Body. I think God is big enough, holy enough, wise enough, and expansive enough to meet us each on the common roads we all walk, while also taking individual steps with each of us on all our disparate journeys.

And in Luke 24, Jesus threads these individuals' stories together into what we all hold in common: the need to eat, the need to be fed. Because as these friends arrive at their destination, Jesus, still disguised as a regular traveler, acts like he's going on ahead, only to feign surprise and delight when these friends invite him to stay and dine with them. The story continues: "After he took his seat at the table with them, he took the bread, blessed and broke it, and gave it to them. Their eyes were opened and they recognized him, but he disappeared from their sight. They said to each other, 'Weren't our hearts on fire when he spoke to us along the road and when he explained the scriptures for us?'" (Luke 24:30–32, CEB).

They recognized Jesus at last, but not from a specific prayer, moment of creedal affirmation, or reprimand. The Risen Lord is made known to them in the breaking of bread. Jesus instituted the Last Supper, Communion, the Eucharist on the night before he was betrayed and killed. And he fulfills it by eating with his friends with his wounded, raised body.

The way to know Jesus is to break bread with him, and to break bread with his Body here on earth, which is—spoiler alert—*everyone*. The sinners and the saints, the outcasts and the insiders, everyone in the room and everyone outside of it. And even to know the scriptures—which Jesus unfolded for them and set their hearts aflame in so doing—is to know them around a table. So while I don't think Jesus gives us simplistic theological statements we can dispense to ourselves or our neighbors when we find them walking, traumatized, along the road at dusk, I do think Jesus gives us a template for meeting him, for encountering the risen God in all their wounded beauty. We can do this by eating his body together. By being the Body of Christ, in all of our diverse bodies and stories, held together with our common hunger for the God who has been walking with us the whole time.

. . . .

Risen Lord:
    Be known to us in the breaking of bread,
    in the faces of our enemies,
    in the faces of our friends,
    and in our shared bellyache for You.
    We trust You will always feed us with the
        sweet wines and rich foods—
    help us trust You more.
    Thank You for feeding us with Your own life-
        giving love,
    the food and drink of new
    and unending life
    in You,
    our Companion on the road, our Mother, and
        our Home.
    Amen.

32

Doubting, Faithful Thomas

....

> So the other disciples told him, "We have seen the
> Lord." But he said to them, "Unless I see the mark
> of the nails in his hands and put my finger in the
> mark of the nails and my hand in his side, I will not
> believe."
>
> JOHN 20:25

All four Gospels say women were the first to see and preach the
resurrected Christ. There's Mary Magdalene, Mary the mother of
James, Joanna, Salome, "and the other women" (Luke 24:10). *And
the other women.* Were there too many to name? Or were the men
who presumably wrote these Gospels simply too ashamed of the
male disciples' disbelief in these women's story to name them all?

Because where do we find the men, while these womenfolk
were out with ointments in hand to dignify the brutalized body
of their Savior? Hiding. In a locked room.*

---

* It's critical that we pause here to understand why John's Gospel says the disciples are
hiding "for fear of the Jews" (John 20:19). John's Gospel was the last of the four to be
written, and by that time, the community from which this Gospel comes was deeply
entrenched in the work of self-identity: they wanted to distinguish themselves from
their Jewish community because they were emerging as their own religious movement.
So John's Gospel often casts "the Jews" as a monolithic group distinct from Jesus. But

Jesus has been raised from the dead. The cosmos is redeemed. And . . . Pontius Pilate is still governing over Jerusalem. Caesar still sits on the throne. Jews are still under Roman occupation. The disciples have reasons to be afraid.

But is it only the people who betrayed and killed Jesus that they fear? Maybe they're afraid because their whole understanding of who God is has been challenged by seeing God hanging on a cross like a criminal. Maybe they're afraid that what the women said about the resurrection is true, because if it is, this Christ who died and rose again might come to make them pay for abandoning him on the cross. The disciples are locked up, afraid, because they cannot or choose not to believe Jesus has risen. They cannot or choose not to believe God loves them so scandalously.

And yet, when Jesus appears among them in the locked room, his words are not words of anger or admonition or shame. "Peace be with you," Jesus says (John 20:19). He shows them his hands and his feet and his side, he breathes the Holy Spirit upon them, and then he leaves. But not all the disciples are present in this room. We don't know who exactly is there, but we know Thomas "was not with them when Jesus came" (John 20:24).

A week goes by, and now Thomas is back with the crew. We don't know where he was before, but now he's hiding with the disciples. And he gets the moniker "doubting Thomas" because he doubts their story. He says, *Unless I see the wounds in his body with my own eyes, I don't believe he's back.* But when we give Thomas that

---

it's extremely important to remember that Jesus was rooted in Jewish culture and identity, that the new covenant of Christ does not eradicate or undermine the old covenant God made, and that to read John's Gospel without this understanding has led historically to dangerous anti-Semitism.

nickname, we're quick to overlook the fact that *all* these disciples are still in hiding with the doors locked. They have seen the Risen Lord, and still they remain huddled in this house! Clearly, Thomas is not the only one harboring some doubts.

And Jesus appears to the disciples again. But this time, Thomas is with them. Thomas, who has said he can only believe their wild story if he himself sees the holes in Jesus's hands and feet. Once again, Jesus does not admonish or shame, but says, "Peace be with you" (John 20:26). And Thomas beholds the man whom he has loved and followed, battered and dead but now *alive*. Thomas sees the holes in Jesus's hands and feet where the nails went in. The gaping wound in Jesus's side where he was stabbed and blood and water came pouring out.

Thomas said he needed to see for himself. Jesus, standing in front of him, does him one better. "Put your finger here," Jesus says, taking Thomas's hand and letting him touch the wounds on his palms, feel the gash in his side (John 20:27).

Was Thomas afraid of what Jesus's reaction would be? First he had abandoned Jesus, and then he'd doubted him. But Jesus takes Thomas's doubts and puts them right in Jesus's own most tender places.

Because God takes our most anguished doubts and questions and touches them to God's own most vulnerable places, and says: *You belong here.* When we question the reality of God. When we doubt God loves us. When we are dubious we can ever be forgiven, included, seen, or wanted. When the anxiety slinks in, bit by bit, until every thought is colonized by panic. When we question the religion we were handed, or the faith we have always known. God is not shaking Her head in disappointment: God invites us right into that wound and puts our hands where it hurts, because God wants us to know there is nowhere we will ever go without Her.

"My Lord and my God!" Thomas cries when he touches Jesus's wounds (John 20:28). Because doubting Thomas is full of faith. His doubts do not mark him as incompetent, unfaithful, or bad. His doubts make his faith his own.

Anne Lamott writes, "The opposite of faith is not doubt, but certainty." There is no faith without doubt. If we are ironclad certain about some aspects of God, I think that's encouraging—but if we're that certain about *everything* . . . we might be playing God, not following God. To paraphrase Saint Augustine, if you think you understand God, then what you understand is not God. Faith takes risk. Love takes risk. Certainty is scarce; courage is needed.

God takes our doubts, along with Thomas's, and says, "Blessed are those who have not seen and yet have come to believe" (John 20:29). He does *not* say: *Blessed are those who have not seen and don't have any doubt.* Blessed are those who *believe*, who cannot always know with our eyes but know with our courage and our risk and our willingness to trust that God will take our pain and hold it right where He, too, is bleeding.

. . . .

God of Life,
    You took Thomas's doubts,
    and absorbed them into the scars on Your body.
    Take now our doubts, our fears, our anxiety,
    and extend over them Your healing touch,
    so that we can be free
    in the knowledge that we do not have to know,

we do not have to understand,
we do not even have to see—
because You do.
And You are with us.
Amen.

33

Things We Cannot Heal

. . . .

I am weary with my crying;
  my throat is parched.
My eyes grow dim
  with waiting for my God.

PSALM 69:3

We do not heal from everything. Some things are so horrific, so life-altering, that even though we keep living, our wounds remain open. Unhealed. To say this as a priest who offers healing liturgies—who follows Christ our true Physician, the one who restores sight and raises the dead—may seem . . . contradictory, at best.

But the thing is, Christ himself is a wounded healer whose very resurrected body still bears the wound in his side and the holes in his hands and feet. Wholeness after trauma does not mean unblemished ease. Bodies are changed. Lives are fundamentally never the same. Perhaps healing means learning to walk even without stability. Perhaps it means adapting to life with a wound, a chronic illness, a chronic despair that threatens to overwhelm us.

I have lived through such a loss—several, in fact, some of which I have shared with you in this book. (Thank you for holding them with me. A sorrow shared may not always be a sorrow halved, but it is one that is less heavy.) After the plane crash that killed several members of my family, there were moments of joy—my wedding to my husband, Jonathan, being the highlight for me and many in my family, I think. But in the wake of our wedding, there settled around me a dullness. An ache that gnawed at my will to live, that made me bitter.

That trauma was eating me from the inside out. And some of it I learned to deal with in therapy, some of it I screamed out in a trauma-informed yoga class, some of it wore down over time, but some of it I just had to accommodate. I had to rearrange my life, my faith, my body to make room for the sadness that would not go, that haunted every July, that tinged every family gathering with the knowledge of who was not there.

And one prayer kept coming to me, over and over: *This may not get better, but I will get stronger.* Not stronger in the sense of white-knuckling my way through grief, growing a hard shell to keep hurt at bay. Not stronger in that I could be grateful for what my loved ones endured. Stronger in that I could bear this hole in my heart, my body, my life.

I became stronger in the same way I now know my body became stronger after giving birth: changed, but here. I will never have the body I used to have, and I don't want it. I don't want my body to look like nothing changed. I made a whole person. My stomach sags, and the stretch marks bloom in a garden on my legs because my power, my love, expanded to make lungs, to weave a brain, to sustain a new life. I don't want a body that does not tell that story.

But I do want a body that hurts a little less, a body that will last. So I do my pelvic floor physical therapy, and I take my long walks, and I learn how to use muscles that a surgeon sliced open.

This healing is essential, but it is not linear, and it is not about restoration to a mythic, perfect state.

Christ defeats death, and he still is marked by its claws: the marks in his hands, his side, his feet. Even God knows what it is to bear the absence of what once was for everyone to see. But God also shows us in this wounded healing: You can, and you will, still live a joy-filled and beautiful life. The thing that tried to kill you, that did kill a part of you, is not the end of the story. Your love is not a limited resource. Your love is not shortchanged by what was taken from you. God has wept with you, and God will rejoice with you, too.

Beloveds, I know the shrapnel from trauma like this can cause as much harm as the event itself. Be merciful with yourself. But also know this: the Big Bad Thing that happened? There will be days it still brings you to your knees, but I know from experience that you will learn when you need to honor this grief by staying down and when you need to honor it by getting back up again.

This healing and non-healing together has made me softer and more tender and more fragile. This is part of my superpower. I can be completely broken and keep living. And so can you.

Because Christ lives, I live. You live. We live. Wounded, and whole.

. . . .

Wounded healer,
    who has wept and walked where we walked,
    who sees what no one else sees,
    who laments what we cannot even name—
    thank You for seeing. For knowing. For being.
    Be with us in the great despair.

Show us the contours of the pit because You
    have been there, too,
and when we are ready
(or maybe when we think we're not),
show us how to climb up,
with shaking limbs and all.
For You are the redeemer of the lost,
    and the healer of the broken,
      and the One who shows us that life is worthwhile,
        even with the holes in the story.
        Amen.

PART IV

The Great Hereafter

MYTH: Christianity is all about securing our ticket to heaven, lest we roast eternally in the flames of hell.

MYSTERY: Jesus spoke about the kingdom of heaven coming near and breaking in all around us; perhaps Christianity is about helping us pay attention to God interrupting and blossoming here on earth.

Most of my closest friends from my life prior to going to divinity school would not identify themselves as Christians. There are some key exceptions to this rule, but until I was ordained, most people in my community were either agnostic, Jewish, or only nominally Christian in that they periodically went to church to appease a relative. To be super clear, these friends have been nothing but supportive of my call to be a priest, and when I started preaching at my church once a month in college, all my friends were in the pews (sometimes even when hungover) to cheer me on. But it does make me, their friend the *priest*, a very atypical presence in a lot of their lives.

Once, at a wedding, a friend chuckled as she told me her partner had asked—with genuine curiosity and concern—how, exactly, I could be a Christian in pursuit of ordination as a priest while being so vocally queer and affirming. "Like, isn't that fundamentally not allowed in her religion?" he'd asked. A few years later, while sipping seltzers on Cape Cod, I completely flabbergasted another friend's partner when I said, "Well, not going to hell isn't really the whole point of Christianity." He shook his head in disbelief and told me—again, so earnestly—that this was mind-boggling to process.

This is . . . a bummer. I mean, it's great that these friends felt comfortable enough to ask me elephant-in-the-room questions; I cherish that trust. But it's a bummer that my faith—something that has given my life such purpose, joy, fulfillment, community, and a commitment to compassion for all people—has such a reputation for ugliness. For being so obsessed with the afterlife that what we do on earth is reduced to a certain set of acceptable behaviors.

I am a priest in the Episcopal Church, which is not a denomination exactly known for fire-and-brimstone preaching. And yet, even if we don't cosign ideas about eternal conscious torment, our silence on the subject has ceded the authority on the matter to scary billboards asking, *If you died tonight, where would you go?*

A powerful myth has grown out of a mix of culture, theology, literature, and scripture. The myth is that Christianity is 100 percent about *not going to hell.* This myth is alluring because it is so scary and, honestly, scary stories hook us in. Alluring, too, because, in the Bible, Jesus talks plenty about accountability, judgment, and burning away the chaff from the wheat.

But the truth is Jesus talks a lot more about the kingdom of God being all around us. Jesus talks a lot about justice here on earth in the *numerous* verses about giving away all our possessions to the poor, not exploiting each other, giving up an attachment to earthly riches, and caring for the vulnerable. He also speaks mostly in stories and metaphors. All those details about the circles of hell and ranks of demons? Those are mostly from what we might call "biblical fanfiction," written by authors like Dante and Milton.

In this section of the devotional, we'll make sure we're paying more attention to the Bible than to *Inferno*, and move from the myth of hellfire into the mystery of the kingdom of God.

34

Hell on Earth

. . . .

Indeed, this is the reason the good news was also
preached to the dead. This happened so that, al-
though they were judged as humans according to
human standards, they could live by the Spirit according to divine standards.

1 PETER 4:6 (CEB)

If you took a drive in vast swaths of America and you knew nothing about Christianity except what you saw on billboards, you
could be forgiven for thinking that the *entire* point of Christian
faith, practice, and belief is to be saved from hell. Not the golden
commandment of loving God and loving our neighbors as ourselves. Not believing God chose to dwell in human flesh among us.
Not the literal Bible verses that say: release all debts, feed the hungry, care most for the vulnerable. Just *Be afraid of hell!* in big, bold
lettering.

In popular culture, we hear more about the eternal fires of damnation than anything in the Bible—and hell isn't even in the Bible!
At least, not the version we think of when we think of hell. The
fire, the brimstone, Lil Nas X descending on an enormous stripper
pole to dance on the devil? Like 90 percent of these images are not
found in the Bible at all. They largely come from works of Western

literature like Dante's *Inferno* and Milton's *Paradise Lost*—which are great stories, sure, but they're *fiction*. They're inspired by the Bible but heavily influenced by the authors' agendas.

We also have taken a lot of different Hebrew and Greek words from different parts of the Bible and joined them into what we think is one concept of hell but is actually quite a mishmash of ideas. For example, the King James Version—probably the most popular English translation of the Bible, despite its age and notable translation troubles—often translates both the Hebrew word Sheol and the Greek word Gehenna into English as "hell."

But if we look at the Hebrew word Sheol as it's used in the Old Testament, it's more of a neutral term for a realm of the dead. It has a negative connotation in the sense that it's a bummer to be dead, but it generally isn't seen as a place where wicked people are tormented. This is precisely why the King James Version can't consistently translate Sheol as "hell," even if it wants to. For example, the KJV renders 1 Samuel 2:6 as "The LORD killeth, and maketh alive: he bringeth down to the grave, and bringeth up," whereas the New Revised Standard Version Updated Edition translates the same verse as "The LORD kills and brings to life; he brings down to Sheol and raises up." As this verse demonstrates, Sheol is far more like the grave (which does of course involve the anguish and perils of dying) than our idea of hell as a fiery pit of eternal conscious torment.

Gehenna, on the other hand, refers to a realm of the dead in the context of a real place on Earth. We first meet Gehenna in the book of Joshua, where it is called by its Hebrew name, Ge ben-Hinnom—"the valley of the son of Hinnom"—because it is a literal valley that marks a border between the lands of the tribe of Judah and lands of the tribe of Benjamin. But (*big* content warning here for harm to children) Gehenna becomes a site of horrific trauma and cruelty when the kings of Judah burn their children alive as human sacrifices there. As God says through the prophet Jeremiah, "I did not command [these children be killed], nor did it come into my mind. Therefore the days are surely coming, says the LORD, when it will no more be called . . . the valley of the son of Hinnom but the valley of Slaughter" (Jeremiah 7:31–32). By the time of Jesus, Gehenna came to be a kind of shorthand for a place of the dead, colored by an uneasy sense of human wickedness and divine judgment.

But even with this connotation of punishment for horrific sin, there is not a consistent function of Gehenna in the same sense that there is for "hell" as a fiery cavern ruled by a devil. When Jesus refers to Gehenna in the New Testament, he's talking about a place people know to be hell on earth.

And we too know what hell on earth is like. Manhattan on 9/11. Hiroshima and Nagasaki. War zones and places of genocide. Sites of lynching. Prisons. Unmarked graves at boarding schools. With mass shootings slaughtering lambs on the altar of school desks, schools in America can be a modern-day Gehenna, may God have mercy on us. These are places where evil things happened.

I wonder, too, if you have ever lived through a personal hell here on earth. When the temptation to use a substance was stronger than the willpower for sobriety. When you got the call that cleaved your life into a "before" and "after." When you thought you could trust someone—and you could not. When the test came back positive. When the test came back negative. When a loved one died.

As a priest, I have been with people when they were in hell. In a hospital room. In a funeral parlor. Sitting with cold coffee around a family dinner table, trying to choose hymns for the memorial service while still haunted by the sight of their loved one's body on the bedroom floor. I have been in hell, too, in those same places—funeral homes and desperately quiet houses. In the deep throes of a terrifying depression. In the knowledge that something could have been done to stop this, but either no one did or the people chose not to. In the knowledge that nothing could have predicted or prevented this.

Sometimes hell is right here on earth. We don't need to imagine a thorny staircase or howling furnace to see it. To smell it.

I suspect this is why the allure of believing in an afterlife of hell is strong: because we know firsthand what hell is. We do not need a billboard to tell us that hell is real. But we also need to know that as real as hell is, God is more powerful than even the most devastating, debilitating fires that eat us alive.

There is a line in a very old prayer called the Apostles' Creed that says Jesus "was crucified, dead, and buried: he descended into hell. The third day he rose again from the dead; he ascended into heaven." Personally, I love this line because it reflects a theology called "the harrowing of hell," which basically says that in those three days when Jesus was dead, he went down into hell and set every captive soul free. Hell is empty, and all the souls are alive with God. But, given the shakiness of the very idea of hell, there are some who prefer to say this prayer as Jesus "descended to the dead" instead of "descended into hell."

In any case, I wonder: How does it change our faith to trust that even in the pit of hell, you are not actually alone? How does our faith unravel and renew itself knowing fear does not need to be our motivator? That our God saw you, saw your pain, and was not scornful or vindictive or angry but had clambered down into the pit before you to help push you out?

Because as much as billboard Christianity wants *us* to be afraid of hell, we can be sure that *God* is not afraid of hell. And God will always, always be with us.

. . . .

Harrower of Hell,
  You take back every key that locks us in chains.
  Forgive us our sins.

Help us trust: there is nowhere we can flee from
    Your presence.
  Help us trust: Your mercy is new every
    morning.
  Help us trust: no prison can contain Your
    liberation.

For You are gracious, O Lover of souls,
  And to know You is to know perfect freedom.
  All this we ask through Jesus Christ our Lord,
    the liberator of the dead,
  who lives and reigns with You and the Holy
    Spirit, one God, for ever
  and ever.
  Amen.

· 35 ·

Bundled, Burned, Delivered

·················

Then the righteous will shine like the sun in the
kingdom of their Father. Let anyone with ears
listen!

MATTHEW 13:43

So if hell is not what threatening billboards promise you'll get
for wearing a miniskirt or being gay, why does Jesus talk so much
about "weeping and gnashing of teeth" or "the outer darkness" or "the pit" when he's telling stories about the kingdom of
heaven?

First off: when Jesus speaks in parables, they are not fables like
Aesop's. They're not meant to be easily decoded morality lessons.
Parables are stories, and like any good story, they rely on metaphor
and imagery to provoke us into a new way of encountering ourselves and the world. I'll paraphrase New Testament scholar Amy-
Jill Levine here: listening to parables is an art that requires us to be
open to seeing the world in a different way.

In Matthew 13, Jesus says the kingdom of heaven is like someone who planted some good seeds in his field—but while they
slept, an enemy came and planted weeds right next to those good
seeds. The people who worked the land didn't know weeds had

been planted alongside the good grain until both began to sprout at the same time.

Confused, and maybe sad or angry at how much work was ahead of them because of all these weeds, a servant goes to the landowner and asks, *Didn't you plant the good stuff? Why are there weeds here?* To which the landowner replies, "An enemy has done this" (Matthew 13:28). The servants ask if they should start weeding, but the landowner says, "No, because if you gather the weeds, you'll pull up the wheat along with them. Let both grow side by side until the harvest. And at harvesttime I'll say to the harvesters, 'First gather the weeds and tie them together in bundles to be burned. But bring the wheat into my barn'" (Matthew 13:29–30, CEB).

Listen, I know almost nothing about gardening, but I remember weeding next to my mother in many a North Carolina spring. I *know* you can weed alongside beautiful rose bushes without ripping up the roses (and I also know it is miserable work—sorry, Mom). But for whatever reason, this landowner—and this parable—says: *Don't do the weeding. Let 'em grow, and we'll burn them later.*

If I'm really honest, I have a hard time hearing this parable as a story about gardening and seeing the world anew when all I can hear is the threatening bass voice of a street preacher telling me I will burn in hell for marching in Pride, his towering sign reading JESUS SAVES. Like, yeah, I obviously believe that Jesus saves. But saves from . . . what? If hell is not exactly what we've been sold it to be on fiery billboards, what does Jesus save us from?

Does Jesus save us from the places where we are haunted by the real evil done in the name of God against innocents? Does Jesus save us from tyrants like Herod or Pharaoh, kings who push babies back into raging rivers because they were born on the wrong side of the border? Does Jesus save us from greedy politicians like Pilate, who want to wash their hands of inconvenience and let rabble-rousers hang rather than stick their own necks out to stop mob violence? Does Jesus save us from demonic possession, like a persistent lust for more guns in a nation already armed to the teeth?

What weeds are being burned here? And is this burning supposed to indicate hell? Or is the burning, to quote that great hymn "How Firm a Foundation," a refining fire in which "the flames shall not hurt you / I only design / your dross to consume / and your gold to refine"? Are these the flames that forge us, not damn us?

If it were up to me, I would say there are *clearly* some people for whom there is much to refine. Sometimes, when I consider the insurmountable evil in this world, honestly, I *want* there to be a fire-and-brimstone hell. Sometimes, I want vengeance for the ways I've experienced hell on earth. I think a lot of us do. We crave vindication. Heaven is considerably less attractive if the murderer or rapist or dictator is also there.

But if I move from *wanting* divine, punitive justice to *deciding* that I get to decide who will suffer, this puts me squarely in the same place as the servants who ask the landowner if they should uproot the weeds to protect the good seed. To which the landowner says: *No. That is a task for the reapers, the harvesters, not for you.* And when Jesus (in a rare move) *explains* this parable to the disciples, he is clear: "The harvesters are the angels" (Matthew 13:39). Not human beings.

So as much as I may *want* to be the person who decides who is wheat and who is a weed, as much as I may *want* to be the arbitrator of heaven and hell, none of us—*none of us*—gets to make that decision. This is why I'm ultimately hesitant as a priest to say that there is no hell; I fear making such a declaration means I'm still the deluded decider, trying to play God. However, I do feel comfortable saying this: Eternal conscious torment does not feel true to the character of God to me. It feels more apt to trust that God's love of us and of justice is a love that will hold us accountable for when we have acted against God and our neighbor. My husband Jonathan (who is also a priest, and one very smart cookie at that) says: God's justice is restorative, not retributive.

Jesus says, "The righteous will shine like the sun" (Matthew 13:43). And the sun is bright. Scorching. If something that lives under the sun is not true, and strong, and able to withstand that heat, it burns. And burning is miserable. Accountability is miserable. And I do believe we are held accountable. But even the most unquenchable fires do not turn something into nothing; they leave behind ashes. And we have a belief about ashes in Christianity: Ashes to ashes, dust to dust. It was from the dust that God first wove us, with tenderness and delight and love.

Because, to my everliving frustration, God really *is* merciful. And God is creative. And God seems to be willing to let a weed grow, and be pruned, and be burned, and try again to see what flowers might bloom.

....

Holy God,
  Holy and Mighty,
  Holy Immortal One,
  Have mercy on us.
  We do not love mercy.

We long for the sun to burn away those we find
    unworthy, unwanted.
Forgive us.
Teach us to dream as You dream:
in color,
in possibility,
in undeserved second chances.
Teach us to fuel our anger into change,
our lament into hope,
and our bitterness into blessing.
Keep our feet steady,
knowing that the real arbitrator of justice is
    You,
and Your justice is true.
Holy God,
Judgment of the Nations, to You we pray.
Amen.

· 36 ·

The Kin-dom of Heaven

· · · · · · · · · · · · · · · · ·

He told them another parable: "The kingdom of
heaven is like yeast, which a woman took and hid
in a bushel of wheat flour until the yeast had
worked its way through all the dough."

MATTHEW 13:33 (CEB)

While there are plenty of references in the parables of Jesus to *hell*
(the English word we use for a variety of different Hebrew and
Greek terms such as Sheol and Gehenna), there are far *more* references to heaven. But just as nonbiblical depictions of hell can dom-
inate our imagination, we're susceptible to nonbiblical depictions
of heaven, too. Heaven isn't exactly fat babies on clouds singing
songs. (Well, heaven *is* a fat baby discovering her little voice, but
you know what I mean.) When Jesus talks about "the kingdom of
heaven," more often than not, he's telling a parable about something happening right . . . now.

Mujerista theologian Ada María Isasi-Díaz coined the term *kin-
dom* when talking about the kingdom of God, replacing *king* with
kin, as in "family," to challenge the undergirding assumptions of
empire and patriarchy in the word. As she says, "the word
'kin-dom' makes it clear that when the fullness of God becomes a

day-to-day reality in the world at large, we will all be sisters and brothers—kin to each other." Because the kingdom, or kin-dom, we pray will come is not going to look like the kingdoms of this age. Remember: Jesus was killed by the kings of his age. His kingdom/kin-dom did not look like dominance; it looked like calling outcasts his kin, like turning the world's injustice upside down to show where God was at work in the tender undergrowth. So when we pray for the kingdom/kin-dom of God, we are looking to the future when God will make all things right.

Or are we?

Jesus talks about the kin-dom of God in the form of parables. My favorite parable is this one: In Matthew 13:33, Jesus tells his disciples that the kin-dom of heaven is like a bit of yeast that a woman mixed into three measures—about sixty pounds—of flour until *all* of the flour was leavened. The Greek verb used here is *enkrypto*, like the English word "encryption." This woman is literally folding a secret surprise into the bread with this yeast, and it is enough bread not just for her, not just for her household, but for the entire neighborhood. Have you ever seen sixty pounds of flour? My kitchen couldn't fit all that bread—but a heavenly banquet table could. Because, I suspect, that is part of the glimmer of God that Jesus is offering us with this parable: God's heavenly table is fat with food and people.

Jesus is also making a clever little callback—one might say an *encrypted* message—to an earlier story in the Bible. Not only is three measures of flour an absolutely over-the-top amount of food, it's also the same amount of flour that Abraham asked Sarah to prepare when he was visited by the three angels in Genesis 18. We talked about that story earlier in this devotional: Abraham has been visited by three heavenly strangers, and in a panic he tells his wife Sarah to prepare cakes from specifically *three measures of flour* to welcome them. And while she is in the kitchen, kneading this dough, she overhears the angels prophesying that Sarah, in her postmenopausal body, is going to have her first child. She laughs at this and asks, "Will I now have this pleasure?" (Genesis 18:12, NIV). And God replies: "Is anything too wonderful for the LORD?" (Genesis 18:14). The implied answer being: *No, there is nothing too good for the God of the universe who made our bodies and all that they are capable of receiving and releasing.*

So what does this callback to Sarah have to do with this story Jesus is telling of a woman who, like the kin-dom of God, is hiding yeast in a genuinely astonishing amount of flour? Well, Jewish New Testament scholar Amy-Jill Levine has a theory: "Genesis 18, underlying the parable of the Leaven, is a story about an unexpected, miraculous, mysterious pregnancy." That is, the yeast—the kin-dom of God—is like that baby Sarah so unexpectedly, pleasurably, and divinely conceived. It is a metaphor both for Sarah's pregnancy and for how God plants the kin-dom in surprising, and pleasurable, ways.

Levine writes, "Perhaps the parable tells us that, like dough that has been carefully prepared with sourdough starter or a child growing in the womb, the kingdom of heaven will come if we nurture it." But I'd actually take this one step further: even if *not* nurtured, even if basically left alone, eventually, that leavened dough and that bun in the oven are going to pop out somehow. Of course, ideally, during pregnancy (which I admittedly know more about than bread-baking), you can take time to nurture yourself and the child, paying attention to the slow bubble of life within you. Bread takes time to rise and bake, and babies take time to grow. Yet in the gestation of both bread and babies, one thing is true: from the moment this process begins, something is happening that cannot be undone without great effort. And even if we aren't paying attention—even if we cannot, or will not, slow down and pay attention—still, the ripening happens.

At the same time, that procreation process is also not yet complete. As Dr. Elizabeth Freese and Rev. Angela Tyler-Williams say, "fertilization is not the moment of procreation." As much as we debate about the beginning of life, the reality of reproduction is that it is very messy, especially in those early days, when you're not sure if your body is fertilizing an egg or if dinner just didn't settle right. There is a whole pregnancy, a whole rising of the dough, for this life to be brought to bear.

The incubation of pregnancy can be miserable; it can also be a miracle. You feel like a destroyer and a maker of worlds. Being given the gift of paying attention to the mundane miracle of making life is part of what made me ready to have my baby. I had so many rational reasons to be terrified of birth and parenting, and yet, when I allowed my completely *irrational* love to be the seed, the yeast, for the love I felt for my baby once she was born, those rational fears lost priority status. They still existed, but I was paying attention to something more important: new life.

We have to pay attention to how heaven is already here with a similar leap of faith to sustain us from now until the kin-dom of heaven fully reigns. It's not in tidy measurements and explicable details—it is in the mystery of mercy, the infinitesimal details of DNA, the inexplicable wonder of being alive with God. Describing the kingdom/kin-dom of heaven as the eschatological end of the age, Saint Paul writes that "the whole creation is groaning together and suffering labor pains up until now" (Romans 8:22, CEB). (The

Bible is full of embodied feminine imagery when we pay attention!)

Right now, we are in the pregnancy phase of the kin-dom coming. Some days feel like absolute death. Some days are the miserable, hot summer when all you want to do is wade in a cold pool and let the water hold you. Yet we are also in the miracle phase where our bellies can roll like an ocean as our child turns within us. God is inviting us into a co-creation and procreation with Her to bring about this kin-dom. Because what happens when we live like heaven is here, to touch? To dance with? To change us, change our world? We demand that this world reflect God's intention for all of us.

We don't bring heaven in ourselves; God does that. Heaven is going to come no matter what. Nothing can stop the will of God, who is the ultimate Creator in this great act of procreating. So when we know hell, we can also know heaven. In fractals of perfection, glimmers that linger. In a toddler hurling herself into your arms with reckless laughter. In the moment a friend says something you didn't know you desperately needed to hear and you're suddenly ten times lighter. Heaven is here, in these erupting moments of surprise and abundance. In making sumptuous love. In sharing a delectable meal. In the gentle ease of sitting on a well-worn couch, tucked next to someone whom you don't have to say a word to, if you don't want to.

Womanist Karen Baker-Fletcher writes that heaven is "a fullness of time in which past, present, and future coexist together." The full kin-dom of heaven, I do believe, is beyond what we can fully see and taste and absorb right now. But just as I *know* angels are around us, how those whom we love but no longer see never leave us, I know, too, heaven is tearing down walls all around us. The feast is ready, with more bread of heaven than all of us could eat in one sitting.

. . . .

Sovereign of Heaven:
Your love is extravagant,
Your love is fragrant,
and we long for You.
Fill us with our daily bread,
and fill us with the knowledge
that there is enough bread,
and enough room,
for all to feast at Your heavenly banquet.
Through Jesus Christ our Lord, who lives
and reigns with you and the Holy Spirit,
one God, for ever and ever.
Amen.

· 37 ·

God Is Offensively Generous

. . . .

"Am I not allowed to do what I choose with what belongs to me? Or are you envious because I am generous?"

MATTHEW 20:15

If it's not obvious: I have *big* Overachieving Oldest Sister Energy. I like to get good grades at everything, even though I've been out of school for years now. I am convinced you can be an A+ student at basically anything—for example, by expediently scanning barcodes at the self-checkout kiosk and expertly packing your bags like you've worked at Target all your life. I like to be the first, the best, and the smartest. (Can I get an A+ in self-awareness, too?)

And I went to a college full of like-minded people: Mount Holyoke, a gender-inclusive women's college in western Massachusetts full of high-achieving, academically competitive women and nonbinary/trans people with huge big-sister energy . . . which meant that class registration time put the Hunger Games to shame. It was an outright bloodbath to try to get into our glowingly rated courses with their small professor-to-student ratios. Everyone was assigned certain windows of time in which to register for classes, and one year, by chance, I was assigned one of the very last possible registration times. Someone has to be last, I guess, and I was the tribute for District 12. By the time I could register, there were literally no openings for the courses I needed to stay on track as a sociology major.

As you might imagine, I took this news with aplomb: by sobbing myself to sleep because my life was now over because I was on *waitlists*. And then my friend Carter and I were having dinner, and they said, "You know, one of my professors just emailed our class and said everyone on the waitlist is being admitted. You could take that class, and then we'd get to hang out. It's a religion seminar."

A religion seminar? I was dubious. I was a burned-out pastor's kid.

But Carter, who is also a pastor's kid and *gets it*, said, "The seminar is called Nonviolence vs. Violence, and we're reading the Bhagavad Gita and Gandhi and Thomas Merton and the Bible *and* Martin Luther King Jr."

They knew they had me. I signed up that night.

And this moment? This was a time machine moment. Do you ever have those? Moments that, even though you didn't realize it at the time, altered the course of your whole life, such that if you could go back in a time machine and change them, everything would turn out different? One small conversation of thousands, one class of dozens, but later, you realize: *this changed my life*. This class was one of those. I changed my major from sociology to religion. The professor, John Grayson, became a trusted friend and advisor, and he encouraged me to follow God's call to the priesthood—which I robustly did not want to do at first. Now our God is not a one-chance-only kind of God, so I think I likely still would have ended up an Episcopal priest. But without that class I think my acceptance of that calling might have taken a lot longer.

And when I think about that class, and my late but life-changing arrival there, I think of the ever-famous parable of the laborers in the vineyard. This story goes like this: Jesus tells another story about the kingdom/kin-dom of heaven. He says it is like a landowner who went out early in the morning to hire workers to tend his vineyard. He found some workers, agreed to pay them fairly, and sent them into the vineyard to begin what would be a long, full day of labor. But this landowner didn't stop there. He kept going back to the market square, hiring people at nine o'clock and twelve noon and three o'clock and five o'clock.

And when the day was over, the landowner began by paying those five o'clock workers first—with the same wage he'd promised to the predawn crew. The predawn crew got excited, thinking they were going to get some major extra pay—after all, if the latecomers received one denarius for essentially doing no work at all, imagine how much the early birds would get for a full day's work. Except they didn't. They got paid what was agreed upon, which was the same one denarius as the five o'clock arrivals. Understandably, they were pretty pissed, but the landowner replied, "Friend, I am doing you no wrong; did you not agree with me for a denarius? Take what belongs to you and go; I choose to give to this last the same as I give to you. . . . Or are you envious because I am generous?" (Matthew 20:13–15).

When I hear this story, I like to think of myself as the kind of laborer who'd show up at daybreak in my work boots and overalls, full of big-sister energy and looking for some divine extra credit. And I strongly identify with those first laborers' righteous indignation that they are paid the same as the laborers who came in at five and scarcely worked.

We are all the first laborers sometimes. Maybe we were the first ones who were able and willing to show up, so we did. Maybe we didn't realize more help was coming, so we worked *really* hard and fried our emotional and physical engines. Or maybe we did see help was coming but thought, *I can do this better than anyone else can*, and we worked even harder, expecting high praise. Or maybe we didn't expect a prize at first—we just did our duty, after all— but now it feels a little unfair that other people get to join the party after we've already wiped down the counters and taken out the trash. Or maybe we were just in the right place at the right time, the early birds who got the worm because of a unique blend of privilege and chance, of circumstance and happenstance.

But what kinds of people would we be if we only received generosity and never extended it? What kind of church would we be if I, as the first to arrive on Sundays and unlock the building, said, "Well, I was here first, and if you were here later, you might as well just leave"?

Because while we're sometimes first to the party, all of us—all of us—are also sometimes the last to arrive. Whether we were late or looked over or dejected or afraid, all of us have been late to figure something out or do the right thing.

But our God is not a one-chance-only kind of God.

And *all of us* have been chosen by an offensively generous God who says, *You—you have work to do. You have a purpose that is not being fulfilled.*

Because this story is about God being generous with *everyone*. When we're inevitably the last to the vineyard, when we're the one who needs mercy and forgiveness and compassion, God gives that freely. God is promiscuous with generosity, extending mercy and purpose and compassion to the overlooked and the undervalued, with love for the big sisters and the late arrivals, always with a wide grin that says, *I am so, so glad you could make it.*

. . . .

God of the late bloomers:
    You hold all things in Your perfect time,
    but sometimes, we wish You'd move on our
        schedule.
    When we lament that we were the last to know
    or we're frustrated that no one else could keep
        pace with us,
    give us Your peace,
    and show us how to step into
    Your Divine dance
    keeping time not with the world's hurry
    or with our own metrics of success,
    but with You,
    ever You,
    perfectly out of time,
    perfectly in rhythm.
    Amen.

38

God Is a Bonkers Gardener

. . . .

Consider then the parable of the farmer.

MATTHEW 13:18 (CEB)

In Matthew 13, Jesus describes an unhinged farmer who flings seeds absolutely everywhere. Some of these seeds land on a path and are snapped up by birds; some fall onto rocky ground where they grow fast but have shallow roots, which makes them too weak to survive the heat of the sun. Some of the other seeds end up among thorny plants, which, predictably, crowd out the growing buds. And finally, miraculously? Some seeds end up on good soil and bear fruit. Like, a *lot* of fruit. A ridiculously bountiful harvest.

After hearing this, Jesus's disciples, understandably, ask him, *What's with all the parables, my dude?* And Jesus actually does explain this parable, claiming that the untimely fates of the different seeds are different metaphors for discipleship. The seeds snapped up by birds are snapped up by "the evil one" (Matthew 13:19), while the seeds that sprouted quick and died even quicker on the rocky ground are people who "hear the word and immediately receive it joyfully" (Matthew 13:20, CEB), but "because they have no roots . . . when they experience distress or abuse because of the word, they immediately fall away" (Matthew 13:21, CEB). The seeds among the thorns are people who are choked by the worries of this life or the false attraction of wealth. And lastly, the seeds that, seemingly through no intention of the gardener, end up on good soil? These are the ones who bear a *gigantic* harvest—more than was ever expected.

If you, like me, have encountered this parable before, perhaps you, too, have fretted over ensuring that you are a seed in the "good soil." We don't want to be so rootless that we only love God when the sun is comfortable and fall away when it's blazing. We don't want, God forbid, to heed the radical call of loving our neighbors and enemies but turn tail and run when such a call threatens our social status or financial security. And goodness me, I certainly don't want to be the seed that gets carted off by the evil one because I was living in bad dirt.

But what about people who grow up choked by thorns *not* of their own making? Or people who are scorched by a merciless sun, be it the capricious chance of the world, or the cruelty of people who should have done and known better, or the bitterness of oppression?

This is the danger of treating a parable like a mere morality tale. It's not that simple, actually. The simple read of this story isn't a bad one; it's just incomplete.

Think about the image of the seed that shoots up fast but burns in the sun. We recognize it from when we first get excited about God, or a new church, or even a new friendship or relationship, but then that happiness fizzles out as soon as things get hard, as soon as the honeymoon phase ends and we have to put in the real work of being vulnerable and receiving the vulnerability of others. Relationships, faith, love—these do ask sacrifice of us. Any true love will change us. Any true love will ask us to prune in order to grow. Relationships are not consumer products. Loving people is *hard*, especially loving people you don't like.

And that's actually the real call of the church. It's not to have amazing sermons or incredible community, as lovely as those are. The real work of the church is to break bread with our enemies and be transformed by a God who loves all of us. And sometimes the enemy isn't someone diametrically opposed to your well-being—it's Carol, who annoys the everliving crap out of you but serves on the same ministry team as you. That's the kind of stuff Jesus calls us to do.

The Bible is not actually a Spiritual Soil Self-Improvement Plan. Let us hold two things in our minds at once: (1) it is a good thing to desire and work to cultivate deep roots and good soil, and (2) the Bible is not a "new year, new you" manifestation journal that offers ten steps to being a better person.

This parable really isn't about the soil at all, actually. These are wild stories of a wild God who is bone-achingly in love with all of us. And, as writer and theologian Debie Thomas puts it, "I think we miss something crucial when we read this Gospel text as 'The Parable of the Four Terrains.' Because that is *not* what it is. It is 'The Parable of the Sower.' It is a parable about the nature and character of God."

And God is *real* fast and loose with those seeds, y'all. I may not have a green thumb, but even I know this gardener, this seed-planter, is not methodically farming the land. Because any careful gardener knows seeds are fickle; they need different amounts of water and air and light and warmth, depending on the plant. So perhaps the point of this story, then, is not about the harvest, but about the farmer's willingness to keep planting. God is not care-lessly flinging seeds. No, God is *extravagantly planting* seeds. God is being downright extra and over-the-top with Their sowing of seeds. And you can bet that is on purpose.

The farmer scatters this seed everywhere—on rocky soil and thorny soil and sunny spots and shady spots and in perfectly man-icured gardens—because the farmer is going to keep throwing wide His hands and inviting any ground that is listening to sing, for however long or short the song lasts. And God is not a one-time planter. If anything is clear from the sower's profligate treatment of these seeds, it is that the sower is going to keep planting, over and over, no matter how many times those flowers shrivel or thorns try to stop their blooming.

God will keep planting seeds in all the soils of our lives, in the rich and healthy seasons and in the seasons when we're burned to a crisp. God will keep planting seeds in the seasons when we're choked with the circumstances of suffering and death, and in times when we can close our eyes and feel the sun and say, "What a good day to grow."

. . . .

Womb of Creation,
    You plant seeds without fear of thorns, or
        scorching, or shallow roots.
    Your love for us is thriftless,
    ceaseless even with cost,
    and yet You are infinitely aware
    of all the times we are choked up, burned up,
        and turn away from You.

Teach us to be so extravagantly trusting.
Give us good soil, God, but more than that,
give us trust that You are a good gardener,
untamed, unbridled,
holy and wild,
and wanting us to come home to You.
Amen.

39

Sent Forth from Revelation to Revolution

....

And now, Father, send us out
to do the work you have given us to do,
to love and serve you
as faithful witnesses of Christ our Lord.
To him, to you, and to the Holy Spirit,
be honor and glory, now and for ever. Amen.

THE POST-COMMUNION PRAYER

At the end of every service in my church, we say a prayer that is helpfully entitled the Post-Communion Prayer. (Seems like a missed opportunity for a Latin pretension.) Many liturgical churches do this, and this prayer we say is very common in the Episcopal Church.

We thank God for feeding us with "spiritual food" and "for assuring us in these holy mysteries that we are living members of the Body of your Son." I've always liked that holy mysteries are what *assure* us of something as uncontainable and liquid as being living participants and limbs of the Living God. It makes me think of that great Fanny Crosby hymn: "Blessed assurance, Jesus is mine!

Oh, what a foretaste of glory divine!" Assurance is another word for promise, for knowledge that moves beyond doubt.

But, as we have learned, doubt is a critical friend and tool in the walk of faith. So why do I find assurance or promise in holy mystery? How can a mystery, something that inherently has no conclusive answer, be reassuring?

Orthodox theologian and bishop Kallistos Ware writes, "It is not the task of Christianity to provide easy answers to every question, but to make us progressively aware of a mystery. God is not so much the object of our knowledge as the cause of our wonder." Holy mystery does not mean we forever stay in the cloud of unknowing and panic at the darkness. It means we know that we will never fully understand all that is to be understood, and we do not *need* to fully understand. We are to wonder, to stand in awe, and to give to God what we cannot carry ourselves.

We also do not carry the weight of faith in isolation. To be a Christian is to be connected to other people—it is not a private spiritual practice but a communal calling. To be Christian is to be a human needing other humans and knowing we need God. As Archbishop Desmond Tutu wrote, "We are bound up in a delicate network of interdependence because, as we say in our African idiom, a person is a person through other persons."

God loves you, and God loves me, but the Body of Christ means God loves us, the big *us* of humanity. Because to be in the Body of Christ is, yes, to love Jesus with our individual body-and-soul (for these things are connected. But more than that, to become the Body of Christ is to become what we eat: to be the individual body-souls made into one whole Body, transcending time and space. Sometimes we call this connecting with the communion of saints.

Our individual bodies together make up the Body of Christ.

Your individual body does not need to shoulder the entire weight of faith. Borrow some of mine, for I will surely borrow some of yours on my lean days. God knows this: it's why God made human beings, not just one human. We need each other. This is also why each of us is made in the image of God: because God knew to plant little seeds in all of us that would make a vibrant garden in riotous, sometimes incongruous colors. This is why Saint Paul says, "All the parts of the body are one body . . . if the foot says, 'I'm not part of the body because I'm not a hand,' does that mean it's not part of the body? If the ear says, 'I'm not part of the body because I'm not an eye,' does that mean it's not part of the body? If the whole body were an eye, what would happen to the hearing? And if the whole body were an ear, what would happen to the sense of smell?" (1 Corinthians 12:12, 15–17, CEB).

We are, all of us, nourished by God's desire *for* all of us. God made us to love us. God loves us in our intimate individuality and also God loves the great us, the royal us that is all of humanity, forever kin-bound as children of God. We are tiny bursts of God's desire breathed into being for the sake of being and of being together. And even tiny revelations are enough for revolution.

That post-Communion prayer ends by saying this: "Send us out now to do the work you have given us to do, to love and serve you." Yes, the church service is over. It's time for coffee hour or brunch or to start your shift at work. These, too, can be places of revolution, because God is as much at brunch as God is in church, and we have been transformed to see God in both places. This is our revelation that can be a revolution: Where will I let God lead me into wonder? Where might I speak for justice and care? What will this stirring up in me lead to, if I let God unfold the next layer? How am I to be merciful? How can I receive God's abundance without fear of the other shoe dropping? How do I care for the more vulnerable parts of the Body with my body?

Because the assurance, the promise, of holy mysteries means that God will change us, if we have the courage to trust that God will be with us when we walk out of the nourishing arms of safety and the known and the easy and into wherever She is calling us. The assurance of holy mysteries means that when we learn something new about ourselves, be it a joy or a drudgery or both, we trust that God already knew and still loves us. And the assurance of holy mysteries means that, by being nourished by the body and blood of Christ as bodies in the Body of Christ, we are fueled for the work. We have eaten our splendid breakfast in time for the long labor in the vineyard ahead.

. . . .

Divine Liberator:
   Thank You for being the One who holds the
      answers;
   remind us that it's more than okay for us to
      have mostly questions.
   Assure us by Your holy mysteries that we
      belong, we are loved,
   and we are ready for whatever is before us—
   with Your help.
   Amen.

· 40 ·

The Great Vigil of Easter

. . . .

The people that walked in darkness have seen a
great light: they that dwell in the land of the
shadow of death, upon them hath the light shined.

ISAIAH 9:2 (KJV)

I find it pretty rude that the more I age, and the more I learn, the
more in the dark I feel. I thought I was supposed to become more
enlightened the older I got. The very word *enlightenment* implies
that to learn something is to be thrown into the light. Enlightenment: living in the light of a new, superior mind.

I suspect, though, that liberation has far more to do with being
plunged into darkness and being okay with opacity than it has to
do with a full-fluorescent experience of the world. Because as
much as the Bible talks about Jesus being the light of the world,
and as much as Christian history has envisioned our salvation as a
city shining on top of a hill or as banishing darkness, the reality of
Easter remains: resurrection happens in the darkness.*

---

* So much of colonialist Christian thinking took imagery of light and read it as "white."
White supremacy, and the brutalizing subjugation of Indigenous people and cultures
in the name of sanctification, is a sin against God and one another. I would be remiss

As it was on the first day, the new day of Christ begins with the evening. As our Creation account told us from the first words of the Bible: *The day, the new, has always begun in the evening.*

"In the beginning," Genesis starts, "when God created the heavens and the earth, the earth was a formless void and darkness covered the face of the deep. . . . Then God said, 'Let there be light'; and there was light. And God saw that the light was good, and God separated the light from the darkness. . . . And there was evening and there was morning, the first day" (Genesis 1:1–5, NRSV). The day God makes begins at night.

God is perhaps most creative in the blackness: in the void over the face of the deep, in the womb, in the knitting together of our inmost parts, in that time where the sun has gone to bed and our dreams awaken and the terrors are real—but so, too, is possibility. In darkness, God is blooming.

But the women who went to meet their Lord were, at best, uncertain of this divine blossoming. Before the light of the first day of the week, Mary Magdalene, Salome, Joanna, Mary, and the other women find one another in the late darkness, the early dawn. Maybe they find one another with furtive glances on the road to the tomb, silently stealing past centurions along the city gates. Maybe these centurions were the same guards who beheld the mockery Jesus made of their armor with palm branches, the way he scorned their weapons by riding a mother donkey with her colt.

---

if I did not explicitly state here that to reclaim darkness is also to reclaim a narrative that white supremacy deliberately obscured in theology, scripture, and discipleship in the name of the idolatrous god of racism.

The women gather in the way we are taught to gather when there has been a death; even in traumatic times, someone has to wipe down the countertops and put food in the refrigerator. Except instead of casseroles, these women have prepared ointments they intend to use to anoint Jesus's corpse. These women walking in the darkness are probably not fearless, but they are going to plunge their way into this early dawn, and they are going to meet their Lord. They just don't know it yet. Until a dazzling stranger appears, shining so bright the guards shake with fear and run away but the women remain unmoved, ready to face whatever fresh hell this may be—and the stranger declares: *Hell is empty. He is not here but has been raised. Go to Galilee. He will be there.*

And the women set off for the miles and miles it will take to reach Galilee, when Jesus interrupts their journey. I imagine his grin goes ear to ear, and with a cheeriness that does not read the room, he bellows, "Greetings!" (Matthew 28:9). He's not trying to be quiet—those centurions are scared of his glittery heavenly friends.

And then perhaps he takes in the shock and trauma and disbelieving belief of the women who had come ready to anoint a corpse and instead beheld him whole—still wounded, but here. So he says, "Do not be afraid" (Matthew 28:10). How many times has God said that to them? To us? How many times throughout the story of scripture and our lives has God said to "be not afraid" of something we were scared of, something that would harm us? And now, here, Jesus, who endured the trauma and misery and torment of a state execution naked on a tree, says to the women who mourned him, who watched him, stood by him, *Don't be afraid. Peace, beloveds. Peace be with you.*

For in the blooming darkness, God has faced the worst things we do to one another and still comes out saying, *I love you; I am here.*

Resurrection happens while it's still dark. While the trauma is fresh, the wounds not yet healed, the sleep deprivation and exhaustion still lingering. Resurrection does not wait for the dawn.

And yet a new day has begun, deep in the shroud of night, peeling away the cloths that bound our God in death and unfurling them with life that is too strong to be held in chains. Jesus rising from the grave tells us: death does not have the final word. And Jesus shows us: there is nothing so broken, so awful, in our lives that it is beyond resurrection. Jesus rose from the grave so we can, too.

Because Easter begins with the evening.

We do not need to be afraid of the dark, for God has gone into hell and taken back every key. God has emptied the cellars and the monsters under the bed and says: *I AM. I am not afraid of you, nor will you make My people afraid.*

So what do we do as a people unafraid? A people set free from fear for a liberated life? We live into the resurrection. We live without fear. Even when we're so damn terrified we can't stop trembling.

There are so many "good" reasons to be afraid. There is so much in this world that has been, is, and will be evil. Death lurks around every stoplight and in every morgue and in the snap of one poor decision. But death does not have the final word. God defeats death by dying.

So we enter the darkness. Not to shine a light on every monster and examine their feathers and talons (though I hope we have seen some monsters together and found them to be less frightening than when they were lurking out of sight). We enter the darkness because we do not have to have every answer to be free. We only need the truth—and Jesus is the way, the truth, and the life that defeats death.

So peace be with you, beloved. Do not be afraid. Resurrection happens in the dark. Resurrection happens at the limits of our knowing, in the surrender of our certainty, in the willingness to be wrong and be righted and be held in it all. Freedom comes when we are okay with walking forward without knowing the full path, because we trust that we do not walk alone. By light and by night, in the known and in the wild yet unseen, we never, ever walk alone.

It is time for us to part, at least for a while, to do the work God has given us to do. In my tradition, we do not close church with a prayer as such. Instead, the priest offers a blessing, and then the people respond. So here is my blessing for you, inspired by the words of Saint Julian of Norwich and the blessing I offer most Sundays at my church, Jubilee:

. . . .

God never promised things would be easy.
  God never promised we would never be sick,
  never be sad, never be lonely,
  never be tired, or never be harmed.
  But God did promise:
  we will not be overcome.

Remember:
  when the storm is raging, God is the shelter;
  and when we are too sheltered, God will bring a
    storm.

So the blessing of God be upon you, now and
     always
   in the name of the Father,
   and in the name of the Son,
   and in the name of the Holy Spirit, One God;

Amen.

Alleluia, Alleluia! Go in peace, to love and serve the
Lord.

And the people respond:
   Thanks be to God; Alleluia, Alleluia.

ACKNOWLEDGMENTS

The village that has raised me, and raised this book, is gorgeous and globe-sprawling. Thank you to my friends, family, teachers, mentors, colleagues, bishops, and parishioners who have each left their mark on these stories and on me. I am blessed to be so loved and to love you. To the communion of saints, especially Meghan, Connor, Stacey, and Chris: if there is beauty here, it is because we still break bread together every week. I love you, I miss you.

None of this dream would be possible without the beautiful church I get to worship with, Jubilee Episcopal Church in Austin, Texas. I am so thankful to every single person whose mere presence in this community makes this dream of God's come alive. I need to especially say thank you to our Bishop's Committee and staff, and their families, from the fall of 2023 to the spring of 2024: Amber, Nicole, Henley, and Carli; Jennifer and Zoe; Brandy and Kaitlyn; Marina, Quentin, and Cameron; Carly, Jeromē, and Kaleb; Chase; Téa; Noel; Helen; and Kim. Your generous leadership and support enabled me to take on this book project. Thank you, too, to the Mission Amplification team and all who work in the Episcopal Diocese of Texas: your vision and courage inspire me.

To my wonderful agent, Jonathan Merritt: thank you for being the best book-midwife and fiercest advocate. To my brilliant editor, Lauren O'Neal: Your clarity, wit, insight, and support means the world. You elevated this book beyond my wildest hopes. I am so grateful to everyone at TarcherPerigee and Penguin Random House for honoring and uplifting my vision—your talent was a given, but I have been so amazed by your kindness and hospitality! Thank you!

Thank you to the beloveds who read dreams and drafts and whose influence brought this book to life. To all of the Beloved Babes of God on social media who asked me so many questions, who shared their stories of stepping back into churches after seeing me be a twirling goof on

TikTok, and who inspired me to write this book: I hope you hear it as my love letter to you, because you inspired me.

To Rachel Held Evans, gone from our eyes but whose leadership lingers—I trust that you now know your memory is still such a blessing to us all. To Carie Jones, who joined the communion of saints too soon, while I was finishing the final draft: Your encouragement meant the world to me, and your love is still known. Thank you. To Mollee Holloman, you have been my favorite polka-dot-wearing librarian for fifteen years—thank you for your priceless feedback on the first rough draft; to Rush Beam and Erin Lane, your permanent place on my Life Board of Directors means your editorial voices are always first in my head (be haunted and honored in equal measure?); to Rev. Christa Moore-Levesque, your kinship in that November writing marathon was a treasure; to Dr. Sara Misgen, your wisdom on the depictions of hell paired with your love of sapphic poetry makes you my favorite professor I never got to have; to Catherine Wicker for saying Jesus was wounded, not scarred—what a gift you are; to Scott Erickson and Candice Marie Benbow for endorsing the book proposal and inspiring me every day; to Rev. Jacob Breeze for taking all of my off-the-wall theology questions with aplomb; and to Dr. Tony Baker for the page numbers! Also, she does not know me, but I just cannot write a list of gratitude without thanking Dolly Parton for embodying what it means to be sensual and spiritual, smart and sassy. You are my preaching hero!

Thank you to Dr. Arielle DuBose for slaying both metaphorical and literal alligators. Thank you to the endless wisdom enclave that is the Young Clergy Women International community. Thank you to my sage spiritual director, Annalise. Thank you to that pew full of friends in college and now: Carter, Austin, Gina, and Grace. To Carly and Cameron for all the conversations while chasing toddlers—thank you. To Maggie and Aaron for being there in both the lean and the full years—thank you. To Amy and Erik for always being a safe harbor—thank you. Thank you to the badass clergy mamas who left the light on for me to follow: the Reverends Luz Montes, Minerva Camarena Skeith, Mia Kano, Leslie Stewart, Ryan Hawthorne, and so many others.

To Nora, my Padfoot: thank you for always asking the right questions. To my podcast cohost, Rev. Laura Di Panfilo: thanks for putting up with my wildly unscripted antics; our conversations on *And Also With You* mean more than you know. To Rev. Hannah Pommersheim: thank you for talking me off the ledge and telling me to leap in equal measure. To the Reverends Angela and Adelyn Tyler-Williams: thank you for telling me to be bigger and braver, most especially when I'm terrified. And to my dearest Brenna: Thank you for being so proud and so *utterly* undazzled at the same time. Your friendship is a sanctuary that helped keep my faith alive. Thank you.

To my family, most especially to my mother, the lionheart, and to my father, the sky-expander, and to my brothers, my first and forever friends: Thank you for the summers at the library, and for enduring every mediocre sermon, and for knowing you were planting seeds that would bloom in ways you could not predict. And still: you planted and tended, anyway. To Pamela and Grace: thank you for claiming me as your own. To Jenn: your courage gives me courage. To my grandmother, Kathleen, whose faith has endured mountains being made into valleys: your prayers will carry our family for generations. To Ramey Jo, Greg, and Grayson: Thank you for keeping the faith and taking the plunge. This book would not be possible without the hours and hours of childcare you provided—and provided with joy and nurture. The support from everyone in my family is so precious to me. Thank you.

To my Jonathan, my husband, my lover. You have carried my heart in your heart, as I carry yours. It should not surprise me so that you love what I love so dearly, but it continually does. Thank you for loving this book, and for loving me into the version of me that could write this book, and for knowing she was there all along. Your love for me, and my love for you, is in every line.

And to the sweet little Lion who kept me company somersaulting in my womb as I wrote this book, and to our ferocious little Rosebud: There aren't enough libraries of words for how much I love you. May you always make a home in the Garden.

All Glory to God.

Selah.

NOTES

INTRODUCTION

xii **To paraphrase my friend Erin:** Erin S. Lane, *Lessons in Belonging from a Church-Going Commitment Phobe* (Downers Grove, IL: InterVarsity Press, 2014), 14–15.

xvii **In the spirit of:** Audre Lorde, "The Master's Tools Will Never Dismantle the Master's House," in *Sister Outsider: Essays and Speeches* (Trumansburg, NY: Crossing Press, 1984).

xvii **A way to dive into:** Saint Teresa of Avila, *The Interior Castle*, trans. the Benedictines of Stanbrook, ed. Benedict Zimmerman (Gastonia, NC: TAN Classics, 2011), 7–8.

PART I: REIMAGINING GOD

1 **Feminist theologian Mary Daly:** Mary Daly, *Beyond God the Father: Toward a Philosophy of Women's Liberation* (Boston: Beacon Press, 1973). I should add that while I greatly admire this book and it was foundational to my own formation as a feminist and Christian, Daly's legacy of excluding trans women from feminism is antithetical to the feminist movement and to a vision of the very Sisterhood of the Cosmic Covenant she sought. I include her scholarship here because it is good work and I am willing to engage with ideas and people complexly, not as a zero-sum game.

1. A CHAOTIC GOD

5 **"When beginning he, God":** Wilda C. Gafney, "Easter—the Great Vigil," in *A Women's Lectionary for the Whole Church: Year W* (New York: Church Publishing, 2021), Kindle.

2. WE WERE BORN HOMESICK

8 **Sin is not, as my:** Kelli Joyce, "What Is Sin?," interview by Laura Di Panfilo and Lizzie McManus-Dail, *And Also With You*, March 4, 2024, https://andalsowithyou.simplecast.com/episodes/what-is-sin.

10 "our hearts are restless": Saint Augustine, *Confessions*, trans. Henry Chadwick (New York: Oxford University Press, 1991), 3.

3. FOOL'S GOLD

12 As novelist Lisa Kleypas: Lisa Kleypas, *Devil's Daughter* (New York: Avon Books, 2019), 312.

5. GOD GAVE YOU THAT BEAUTIFUL BODY ON PURPOSE

22 And these changes are not: Esther Hugenholtz, "The Magic of Mikveh—Transition & Transformation," A Small Sanctuary, September 24, 2023, YouTube video, 17:29, https://www.youtube.com/watch?v=cd6J-0N0W68.

6. EVE'S QUESTION

26 And the snake says: Robert Alter, *The Five Books of Moses: A Translation with Commentary* (New York: W. W. Norton, 2008), 24.

27 Eve sees the fruit: Alter, *Five Books of Moses*, 24.

29 a lot more than crime and punishment: Patrick S. Cheng, "Introduction," in *From Sin to Amazing Grace: Discovering the Queer Christ* (New York: Seabury Books, 2012), Kindle.

29 As my friend Candice: Candice Marie Benbow, *Red Lip Theology: For Church Girls Who've Considered Tithing to the Beauty Supply Store When Sunday Morning Isn't Enough* (New York: Convergent Books, 2022), 93.

9. HAGAR, THE ENSLAVED WOMAN WHO NAMED GOD

44 "So Hagar named the Living": Wilda C. Gafney, "Advent II," in *A Women's Lectionary for the Whole Church: Year B* (New York: Church Publishing, 2023), Kindle.

45 Hagar the first woman: Gafney, "Advent II."

46 "a power attributed to no one else": Phyllis Trible, *Texts of Terror: Literary-Feminist Readings of Biblical Narratives* (Philadelphia: Fortress Press, 1984), 18.

46 "Was Hagar's naming of God": Delores S. Williams, "Hagar's Story: A Route to Black Women's Issues," in *Sisters in the Wilderness: The Challenge of Womanist God-Talk* (Maryknoll, NY: Orbis, 2013), Kindle.

47 "a black feminist": Alice Walker, *In Search of Our Mothers' Gardens: Womanist Prose* (New York: Harcourt Brace Jovanovich, 2004), xi.

10. JOSEPH'S FABULOUS COUTURE COAT

50 "product of ancient haute couture": Robert Alter, *The Hebrew Bible: A Translation with Commentary* (New York: W. W. Norton, 2019), 139.

52 "The resentment and bitterness": David Marchese, "Alok Vaid-Menon Is 'Fighting for Trans Ordinariness,'" *New York Times Magazine*, July 27, 2023, https://www.nytimes.com/interactive/2023/07/29/magazine/alok-vaid -menon-interview.html.

11. THE BRUTALITY OF MERCY

58 To paraphrase my colleague: Joyce, "What Is Sin?"

12. IS IT EXODUS? OR IS IT TEXAS?

62 Now, as womanist scholar Wilda: Wilda C. Gafney, "Shabbat Shemoth," Womanists Wading in the Word, January 5, 2013, https://www.wilgafney .com/2013/01/05/shabbat-shemoth/.

62 It would not be too: Loretta J. Ross, "Preface," in *Revolutionary Mothering: Love on the Front Lines*, ed. Alexis Pauline Gumbs, China Martens, and Mai'a Williams (Oakland, CA: PM Press, 2016), xvi.

63 And as part of my: "About" (under "Who"), Spiritual Alliance of Communities for Reproductive Dignity (SACReD), accessed May 6, 2024, https://www.sacreddignity.org/about/.

13. JUBILEE: GOD'S JUSTICE IS GOD'S JOY

68 The logic of Jubilee: Alter, *The Hebrew Bible*, 451–56.

14. THE SPIRITUAL DISCIPLINE OF JOY

70 "joy is the most vulnerable": Brené Brown, *Dare to Lead: Brave Work, Tough Conversations, Whole Hearts* (New York: Random House, 2018), 81.

70 Joy is so incredibly vulnerable: Brown, *Dare to Lead*, 81.

72 "Keep watch, dear Lord": Episcopal Church, *The Book of Common Prayer* (New York: Church Publishing, 1979), 71.

16. BORN IN DAZZLING DARKNESS

81 To paraphrase Rowan Williams: Rowan D. Williams, "The Body's Grace," in *Theology and Sexuality: Classic and Contemporary Readings*, ed. Eugene F. Rogers Jr. (Oxford: Blackwell, 2002), 309–21.

82 Theologian Sarah Coakley makes: Sarah Coakley, *God, Sexuality, and the Self: An Essay "On the Trinity"* (Cambridge: Cambridge University Press, 2013), 139.

83 **Advent, the church season:** Cole Arthur Riley (@blackliturgies), Insta-
gram post, November 27, 2023, https://www.instagram.com/blacklitur
gies/p/C0KDLQwOZ3p/.

83 **As Sojourner Truth said:** Cynthia Greenlee, "The Remarkable Untold
Story of Sojourner Truth," *Smithsonian*, March 2024, https://www.smith
sonianmag.com/history/remarkable-untold-story-sojourner-truth
-180983691/.

84 **It is a question:** I am indebted to Rev. Ben Maddison for this insight and
for this article: Ben Maddison, "Mary Definitely Knew," *Mockingbird*, December 21, 2018, https://mbird.com/religion/mary-definitely-knew/.

17. MOTHER OF GOD, DETHRONER OF DRAGONS

92 **Religious scholar Lauren Winner writes:** Lauren F. Winner, "Blessed Are
Mary, Judith, and Yael," *The Christian Century*, December 17, 2015, https://
www.christiancentury.org/blogs/archive/2015-12/blessed-are-mary
-judith-and-yael.

19. BACKWOODS EMPIRE

102 **Pull aside the tinsel:** The line "under the rubble" here is a direct reference
to the words of Rev. Munther Isaac. Monjed Jadou, "'If Christ Were Born
Today, He Would Be Born under Rubble, Israeli Bombing,'" *Al Jazeera*, December 7, 2023, https://www.aljazeera.com/news/2023/12/7/if-christ
-were-born-today-he-would-be-born-under-rubble-israeli-bombing.

20. JESUS LOVES A SLOPPY DISCO

104 **If ever you doubt:** For this language of "truly God and truly human" instead
of "fully God and fully human," I am grateful to my friend and colleague
Rev. Jacob Breeze. You can hear more of him speaking about this on Season 1, Episode 11 of my podcast *And Also With You*, "Who Is Jesus?," https://
andalsowithyou.simplecast.com/episodes/who-is-jesus.

21. BEING BORN AGAIN IS ABOUT BEING A BABY

112 **In her book *Revelations*:** Julian of Norwich, *Revelations of Divine Love: Short
Text and Long Text*, trans. Elizabeth Spearing (New York: Penguin Books,
1998), 136.

112 **Or, translated more literally:** Julian of Norwich, *A Revelation of Divine
Love*, np, manuscript, 1373, *Literature in Context: An Open Anthology*, accessed April 4, 2024, https://anthology.lib.virginia.edu/work/Julian/julian
-revelation.

113 As Julian writes: Julian of Norwich, "Canticle R: A Song of True Mother-
     hood," in *Enriching Our Worship 1* (New York: Church Publishing, 1998), 40.

22. THE TENACITY OF A BLEEDING WOMAN

117 But to paraphrase Alice Walker's: Walker, *In Search of Our Mothers' Gar-
     dens*, xi.

23. GOD LOVES US BIGGER

120 To quote my friend: Jay Hulme, "Guest Preacher: Jay Hulme at Jubilee Epis-
     copal Church on November 12, 2023," Jubilee Episcopal Church, YouTube
     video, 108:40, https://www.youtube.com/watch?v=GODvubzQjN0.

24. BAPTIZING THE GENDER-FRINGE

122 Now, our modern ears flinch: Anna Case-Winters, *Matthew: A Theological
     Commentary on the Bible* (Louisville, KY: Westminster John Knox Press,
     2015), 236–41.
123 Still, even within: Case-Winters, 236–41.
124 Eunuchs were people excluded: Case-Winters, 236–41.
124 But *eunuch* could also refer: Emmy Kegler, "Is the Eunuch of Acts 8 Non-
     binary?," Queer Grace, April 28, 2021, http://queergrace.com/nonbinary
     -eunuch/; Elliot Kukla, "Terms for Gender Diversity in Classical Jewish
     Texts," TransTorah, 2006, http://transtorah.org/PDFs/Classical_Jewish
     _Terms_for_Gender_Diversity.pdf; Tony Keddie, "'God Made Them Male
     and Female . . . and Eunuch': Why the Biblical Case for Binary Gender Isn't
     So . . . Biblical," *Religion Dispatches*, May 11, 2023, https://religiondis
     patches.org/god-made-them-male-and-femaleand-eunuch-why-the
     -biblical-case-for-binary-gender-isnt-so-biblical/; Austen Hartke, *Trans-
     forming: The Bible and the Lives of Transgendered Christians* (Louisville, KY:
     Westminster John Knox Press, 2018), 101–11.

26. A DRAG QUEEN MESSIAH

132 To paraphrase theologian Fleming Rutledge: Fleming Rutledge, *The
     Crucifixion: Understanding the Death of Jesus Christ* (Grand Rapids, MI: Eerd-
     mans, 2017).
133 "Pilate's procession displayed": Marcus J. Borg and John Dominic Crossan,
     "Palm Sunday," in *The Last Week: What the Gospels Really Teach About Jesus's
     Final Days in Jerusalem* (New York: Harper Collins, 2009), Kindle.
134 To quote theologian Debie Thomas: Debie Thomas, "The Clown King,"
     Journey with Jesus, March 29, 2015, https://www.journeywithjesus.net
     /essays/3637-20150323JJ.

135 **As drag artist Sasha Velour:** Sasha Velour, "Drag Performer Sasha Velour Explains What the Art Form Means to Her," interview by Jeffery Brown, PBS NewsHour, June 20, 2023, https://www.pbs.org/newshour/show/drag-performer-sasha-velour-explains-what-the-art-form-means-to-her.

27. JUDAS GOT HIS FEET WASHED, TOO

139 **As Archbishop Desmond Tutu wrote:** Desmond Tutu, *No Future Without Forgiveness* (New York: Random House, 1999), 271.

139 **We don't forgive good things:** Joyce, "What Is Sin?"

28. BREASTFEEDING THE BODY OF CHRIST

144 **And not just any food:** Angela Garbes, *Like a Mother: A Feminist Journey through the Culture and Science of Pregnancy* (New York: Harper Wave, 2018), 153.

29. GOD'S OWN BODY

147 **"For as the body is":** Julian of Norwich, *Revelations of Divine Love*, 49.

30. THE CROSS WAS A WEAPON

153 **Crucified people died from exposure:** John Granger Cook, "Easter: Crucifixion in the Roman Empire," interview by Dave Roos and Helen Bond, *Biblical Time Machine*, March 18, 2024, https://www.biblicaltimemachine.com/listen-to-episodes/b24fssktgs7yzxz-scarm-bxjxm-jr9y7-khjbb-zn9dd.

153 **"The cross has been transformed":** James H. Cone, *The Cross and the Lynching Tree* (Maryknoll, NY: Orbis Books, 2011), xiv.

153 **"The cross needs the lynching tree":** Cone, *The Cross and the Lynching Tree*, 161.

31. YOU WILL KNOW HIM BY BROKEN BREAD

159 **"God's punishments are also God's blessings":** This is similar to something I heard Anderson Cooper say, quoting Stephen Colbert *to* Stephen Colbert, in a moving interview between them on grief and losing parents. "Stephen Colbert: Grateful for Grief," *All There Is with Anderson Cooper*, CNN Audio, September 21, 2022, https://www.cnn.com/audio/podcasts/all-there-is-with-anderson-cooper/episodes/ae2f9ebb-1bc6-4d47-b0f0-af17008dcd0c.

32. DOUBTING, FAITHFUL THOMAS

165 **Anne Lamott writes:** Anne Lamott, *Plan B: Further Thoughts on Faith* (New York: Riverhead Books, 2006), 256.

34. HELL ON EARTH

177 But even with this connotation: With thanks to Dr. Sara Misgen, a
scholar on hell as a concept in Christianity, for her insight on this particular point! "What Is the Hell?," interview by Laura DiPanfilo and Lizzie
McManus-Dail, *And Also With You*, October 30, 2023, https://andalso
withyou.simplecast.com/episodes/what-is-the-hell.

35. BUNDLED, BURNED, DELIVERED

180 So if hell is not: Sara Misgen, "What Is the Hell?"
180 I'll paraphrase New Testament scholar: Amy-Jill Levine, *Short Stories by
Jesus: The Enigmatic Parables of a Controversial Rabbi* (San Francisco: Harper-
One, 2014), 4.

36. THE KIN-DOM OF HEAVEN

185 "the word 'kin-dom'": Ada María Isasi Díaz, *Mujerista Theology* (Maryknoll, NY: Orbis Books, 1996), 103.
186 The Greek verb used here: Levine, *Short Stories by Jesus*, 131.
187 Well, Jewish New Testament scholar: Levine, *Short Stories by Jesus*, 136.
187 "Perhaps the parable tells us": Levine, *Short Stories by Jesus*, 136.
188 "fertilization is not the moment": Elizabeth M. Freese and Angela Tyler-
Williams, "Justice Alito's Bad Theology: Abortion Foes Don't Have 'Morality' on Their Side," *Salon*, July 26, 2022, https://www.salon.com/2022
/07/26/justice-alitos-theology-abortion-foes-dont-have-morality
-on-their-side/.
189 Womanist Karen Baker-Fletcher writes: Karen Baker-Fletcher and Garth
Kasimu Baker-Fletcher, *My Sister, My Brother: Womanist and Xodus God-Talk*
(New York: Orbis, 1997), 286.

38. GOD IS A BONKERS GARDENER

198 "I think we miss something": Debie Thomas, "The Extravagant Sower,"
Journey with Jesus, July 5, 2020, https://www.journeywithjesus.net
/essays/2687-the-extravagant-sower.

39. SENT FORTH FROM REVELATION TO REVOLUTION

201 "And now, Father": Episcopal Church, *The Book of Common Prayer*, 366.
202 Orthodox theologian and bishop: Kallistos Ware, *The Orthodox Way*
(Yonkers, NY: St Vladimir's Seminary Press, 1979), 14.
202 "We are bound up in": Tutu, *No Future Without Forgiveness*, 35.

40. THE GREAT VIGIL OF EASTER

206 **God is perhaps most creative:** See Saint Gregory of Nyssa and "the daz-
     zling dark" in *The Life of Moses*, Sarah Coakley's *God, Sexuality, and the Self*,
     and the collected works of Rev. Wilda C. Gafney.

209 **So here is my blessing:** "And these words, 'You shall not be overcome',
     were said very loudly and clearly, for security and comfort against all the
     tribulations that may come. He did not say, 'You shall not be tormented,
     you shall not be troubled, you shall not be grieved', but he said, 'You shall
     not be overcome.'" Julian of Norwich, *Revelations of Divine Love*, 34.

ABOUT THE AUTHOR

© Riley Glenn Photography

Rev. Lizzie McManus-Dail, a.k.a. "Father Lizzie," is the vicar of Jubilee Episcopal Church in Austin, Texas, which she planted in 2022. Known online for her trademark phrase "beloved babes of God," she uses her social media platform to unravel toxic theology and reveal the abiding love of a joy-full God. She lives with her husband, Rev. Jonathan, and their two beloved daughters, who are often found on Lizzie's hip or underfoot while she preaches.